Why
Scottish
History
Matters

EDITOR
Rosalind Mitchison

Why Scottish History Matters

with essays by
Geoffrey Barrow
A A M Duncan
Alexander Grant
Michael Lynch
David Stevenson
Bruce P Lenman
T M Devine
R H Campbell
Christopher Harvie

First published 1991 by The Saltire Society
This revised edition published 1997 by
The Saltire Society,
9 Fountain Close,
22 High Street, Edinburgh EH1 1TF

A catalogue record for this book is available
from the British Library.

ISBN 0 85411 070 4

Designed by Mitchell Graphics, Glasgow

Printed and bound in Scotland by Bell & Bain Limited

Contents

The Purpose of this Book

For an individual the destruction of memory means the destruction of personality. Human beings are the product and embodiment of their own past. It is only by contact with this past, in thinking and in relationships, that we exist. The same is true for societies: their history is the main component of their present identity. History also provides useful lessons and warnings to governments of the kind of mistakes they are particularly prone to, but its main significance is in enabling us to know ourselves. This book is an affirmation of the importance of history to the world of today.

But what history? What kind of history and of what social, economic or political units? The habit of the past, fortunately never an exclusive habit, was to think of history as political, constitutional and legal, and therefore exclusively the history of independent states. Economic history was a minor but recognised genre. Social history was the study of the domestic life of the nobility, medical history the major discoveries of the working of the human body, local history a look at surviving buildings, families or the ownership of land. Today we have widened our ideas and recognise a much greater range of what counts as history, and in particular acknowledge that the bulk of the common people have had their own history in social structure, mechanisms for survival, conventions and beliefs. We are now aware that there are separate histories of separate peoples within the nation states. For those who live within the British Isles it is reasonable to assume that British history means the history of the separate nationalities which at one time or another have been joined up to make a single state, that is, Scottish, Welsh and Irish, as well as the politically dominant English. It should also include a recognition of a part played within a wider world and the influences from that world. British history cannot ignore the community of states round the North Sea, the nations of Western Europe, the Mediterranean world, the links across the Atlantic, the British Commonwealth. All these have played a part in the British story, and in the individual stories of the components of

1

Britain, as they still do. But it would be reasonable to expect that the weight of history studied in any one country would be the history of that country.

In practice for most of the last hundred years this has not been the kind of history that has been offered in formal education to the young of Scotland. There has been very little Scottish history in the experience of school children, beyond stories about Robert Bruce and other monarchs and some naming of battle sites. Some prejudices, particularly those shown in Sir Walter Scott's *Tales of a Grandfather*, have also been incorporated. But otherwise history has mainly meant English history. In English schools British history has almost always been the history of England, with diversions to glance at other parts of the British Isles when these were upsetting the smooth action of the English political system. Since it has mainly been Ireland that performed this function, a greater proportion of the small attention paid to the other parts of the British Isles has gone to that country than has been available for Scotland or Wales, and Scotland's small share has been greater than that of Wales.

The reasons for this concentration of attention are themselves historical. The time of the development of Honours schools of History in most Universities coincided with a new significance of examination in entry to the Civil Service. Historians have usually been valued by the Civil Service since they have been trained in the kind of decision-making that is appropriate there. The advanced state of English historical research at that time meant that high-quality history was seen to be synonymous with English: in particular it was based on the voluminous archive produced by the highly bureaucratic and centralised government of mediaeval England interpreted by a series of brilliant historians. The other countries could not compete. That since then these have developed new ways of looking at their own documentation, recognising that it fills some holes that the Public Record Office in London cannot, has not changed this emphasis of historical study, for the teachers in the schools of the Celtic fringe were trained in the same courses as the prospective Civil Servants.

Particularly over the last twenty five years there has been a resurgence of research and study in the history of these countries, and an impressive range of published works. In the case of Scottish history this has over-ridden the somewhat stereotyped image of the country's past imposed by over-ready acceptance of the historiography of the presbyterian churches. New types of history and new approaches to accepted types have flourished. These facts remind us that historians cannot rest on any one generation's achievements: history itself is an area of historical development.

Scotland is, and has been, a small country in terms of power and population, situated on the periphery of Western Europe, in the culture of which she has shared. The distinctiveness of her history stems from her location, the mixture of the peoples that have settled her, her changing relationship to other nations in terms of trade, culture, personalities, migration and war, the particular forms in which Christianity was received and developed, all these. It would be a pity if the study of these features were to be ignored by the curricula of school, college and university.

The writers of the essays in this book do not assert that Scotland's history is better than that of other countries, but that it is different and worthy of study, and particularly relevant to Scotland.

Scotland's sense of national identity has survived the lack of serious study of national history because a limited amount of knowledge of it has percolated through the educational system to most people. Literature, the press, the structure of Scotland's governing institutions in Church and State have reaffirmed its separate character. This book has been designed as a plea that this process should expand, and that people within and outwith Scotland should be enabled to acquaint themselves with the country's particular history. It is hoped too that the current approach to the history curriculum in English schools will include a new type of British history which will involve paying serious attention to the interlocked history of the different peoples of these islands.

It was with these aims in mind that a committee of the Saltire Society asked individual historians of Scotland to write essays on their main periods or topics of research bringing out the dominant interest they found there. Some have directly placed their sense of the importance of Scottish history in their chosen period at the start of their essays, others have entered into the main features they discern in their period and allowed the special national characteristics deserving study to be revealed on reading. All are convinced that Scotland's history is interesting, important, developing and

worthy of study, even if they have not expanded on this point. It is
their hope that this book will help to spread the study of it in
Scotland and elsewhere. To help in this process there is, at the end
of this book, a short bibliography for those who wish to pursue
further study.

This is the second edition of the book. For this four of the essays
have been somewhat enlarged, and so has the list of recommended
reading.

The committee which has edited this book offers its warm thanks
to these historians for their willing co-operation and the generous
gift of their time and effort.

Rosalind Mitchison

Introduction

G. W. S. BARROW

President, Saltire Society, 1987–90; Honorary President 1994–

THE EIGHT ESSAYS which follow amount to a snapshot, taken in the last decade of the twentieth century, of evaluations of the history of their country, and the writing of that history, by a group of prominent and experienced Scottish historians. Inevitably, the attitudes of these writers present contrasts and differences, but they are all agreed that the answer to the question put to them by the Saltire Society, 'Why does the history of Scotland matter?', is important and well worth stating and arguing. The Saltire Society, which decided to put the question to them at the beginning of the 1990s, was founded in 1936 by people who believed passionately that Scottish history *did* matter because it provided the story and explanation of the culture of the Scottish people – their values, language, literature, religious beliefs and practices, sports and pastimes, learning, art and creative imagination. The men and women who founded the Saltire Society and those who have supported it over more than half a century have been concerned lest each succeeding generation, whether still inhabiting the Lowlands, Highlands and Isles of Scotland or scattered far and wide across the world, would turn out to be 'the end of an auld sang', as Chancellor Seafield predicted would be the fate of Scotland itself, subsumed after 1707 within that strange newfangled creature the 'united kingdom'. If, instead of being merged without trace into something quite alien – whether that be the culture of England or of the United States or of Europe – Scots culture has in fact survived, much altered of course, as all but fossilized cultures always are, but nonetheless Scottish, then the history of this culture, the charting of inputs and influences, the assessment of its impact upon non-Scottish societies and culture, the estimate of Scotland's place in Europe or the North Atlantic or even the world at large needs to be studied and understood as the explanation of a living organism. This is how it has been understood by the eight contributors to the book. They have not been attracted by the view, found commonly in England and widely represented in the United States and on the continent of Europe, that both the country and the culture of Scotland were voluntarily and deliberately extinguished by the Scots in 1707, since when the great majority of Scots have migrated to other lands (especially to England and North America) and become absorbed by their nationalities and cultures, leaving only an insignificant residue still located north of Tweed and Solway. On this view, which has been shared by not a few historians teaching in Scottish universities, the history of Scotland is no more than an essay in recherché antiquarianism, proper for a small band of slightly cranky specialists but not to be encouraged among the young. *Why Scottish History Matters* sets out to combat these pessimistic beliefs. Its authors believe firmly that Scotland and the Scots have a real existence, and none of them is in any danger of denying the importance of their history.

The writers of the various chapters approach their task in a buoyant mood. The 'socially and politically peaceful realm' of King Alexander, who died in 1286, was the ancestor of the many Scotlands which have existed since that far-off time. But Archie Duncan demonstrates how that realm had roots going back much further still. The picture he gives is of a fascinating and complex blending of several distinct and in some cases markedly different races, languages and cultures combining to form a recognisable community. Alexander Grant follows this picture of beginnings with an account of a self-confident realm prepared to face severe external challenges. Mediaeval Scots invested a great deal in their long-drawn-out struggle to preserve independence of England and gained much by not being conquered and not being beset by civil wars and violent power-struggles. Michael Lynch points out that in addition to having two Reformations (1560 and 1567) Scotland experienced no fewer than three Renaissances, one for the court, another for the provincial nobility, and yet another (or others) for the merchants and lesser lairds. David Stevenson's seventeenth century saw the vitally important working-out of this sixteenth-century ferment, first of all in the breathtaking over-confidence or arrogance of the upholders of the National Covenant, then by reaction in the despair and self-criticism of the generation which followed Cromwellian conquest. He sees the real significance of Scottish history between 1603 and 1649 as illustrating the problems of a small state within a multiple monarchy. Bruce Lenman shows in turn how the eighteenth century saw the slow working-out of the previous century's issues – dynastic, constitutional, religious and intellectual: resulting in the total defeat of the royal Stewarts; the adoption of incorporating Union with England and with it a corrupt, aristocratic form of collective government; the triumph of the moderates leading eventually to toleration and pluralism; and the marvellous flowering of the Scottish Enlightenment, the antecedents of which lay firmly in the seventeenth century. All this while the economic muscles of Scotland had been stirring, and it is the task of Tom Devine and Roy Campbell to sketch the birth and heyday of commercial and industrial Scotland – the land not of tartan and haggis, but of inventors, engineers, factories, mines, foundries and slums.

Victorian Scotland is a hard act to follow whether you admire it or are scunnered by it. Christopher Harvie has perhaps the most difficult labour of all. He conveys well the living fascination and significance of Scottish history, reminding us of how much has altered even since the 1950s. As we approach the millennium, he suggests that we look at Scottish history from a completely fresh standpoint. No longer should the subject nervously beg for its quota in the history syllabus: 'a European country which contributed so much to the continent's past, and can surely contribute so much more to its future' must surely demand an established position for its history at school and university level, and not feel the need to defend itself at every turn.

Sueno's Stone at Forres: see page 14

The Making of the Kingdom

A. A. M. DUNCAN

Professor Emeritus of Scottish History, Glasgow University

REFLECT ON THE NAME 'Scotland'. It is English in form and in its second syllable, but the first syllable, perhaps meaning 'pirates', was a 'learned' word passing gradually from literary to common use, and not the name used by the Scots (Irish-speaking settlers) in Britain of themselves. We may treasure and be proud of the name Scot and Scotland, but we should be aware that they are both words of relatively recent origin and that 'Scot' described originally only one thread in the varied tapestry of our beginnings. These were the men of Ireland who raided Britain for its wealth in silver in the days of declining Roman rule, when a relatively dense population in northern Europe struggled to survive on resources diminishing as the climate shifted to a prolonged period (about 200–1000 AD) of colder and wetter seasons. Chiefs and even peoples sought other lands and others' wealth in the age of European migrations which brought the Scots to settle in the fourth or fifth century, when they probably brought with them some trappings of the Christian faith and literacy.

The people whom they displaced from Argyll, the Picts, spoke a language which was probably of the same Celtic family as British or Gaulish but we are now careful not to equate language with migration or ethnic origin. If one people has to be identified as ancestor of the modern Scot, then the Picts probably have the best claim to that role: they occupied the lands north of the Forth as far as Unst, but have left us only the record of place-names and the stones carved with cryptic symbols and scenes of battle and hunting which tell us of their appearance and trappings, but not their political or social organisation. Later centuries inherited lists of Pictish kings which modern criticism can edit into one list running from the mid-sixth century till the mid-ninth, but we do not know whether this was the line of one among several kingdoms, of over-kings among sub-kings, or of the only kings in the lands of the Picts. As their very name (in Latin meaning 'painted people') is a puzzle – did it have a different *Pictish* meaning? – so their kings ask us more questions than they answer.

And to these we must add the puzzle of the 'union' of Picts and Scots. If the phrase conjures up for the reader a proto-James VI on the high road from one kingdom to another, or two parliaments passing acts of union, then he should cast away the vision. The kingdom of Alba, of Picts and Scots, may have been formed because of some dynastic claim: it was more probably the result of victory by the war-band of one provincial chief over the bands of other chiefs, both Pictish and Scotic. In contrast with the wealthy kingdoms of southern England, the rulers of Alba struggled for mastery of a moneyless and economically peripheral land. Their resources were the estates belonging to the king and the right to command all men to serve in the host for the defence of the land.

The need for that defence was pressing after the 790s when the first Norse raiders appeared on the western seaboard. Probably they had already settled Shetland and Orkney, which formed an earldom loosely under the Norwegian crown until 1468–9, when, in effect, sovereignty was recovered by Scotland. The Western Isles, on the route to the wealth of Ireland, also attracted these settlers, most thickly in Lewis, fewer as the isles became more southerly. From about 1100 these islands (with Man) formed a Norse-Gaelic kingdom also under the Norwegian crown, until 1266 when they were ceded to Alexander III king of Scots after he had shown the capacity to conquer them.

But the Northern and Western Isles were peripheral to the development of mainland Scotland, for they were isolated by mountain and sea from the wealth-producing straths and plains south and east of the Highland Fault. Although the tools and techniques of agriculture were primitive by modern, and perhaps by later mediaeval, standards, the grain-producing soils of the Lowland zone (broadly interpreted) supported the densest population and therefore the wealthiest lordships.

That zone was divided by the River Forth and its Firth. The great moss stretching west from Stirling remained the single greatest barrier dividing the isle of Britain until it was drained in modern times – a barrier to invading armies of Romans or English, but also to migrating peoples, the British in prehistoric times, the Angles from the sixth century. This Anglian migration was probably of a dominant aristocracy only, but the language of the conquered British tribes between Humber and (West Lothian) Avon yielded to the speech of the conquerors. Only to the west, in Cornwall, Wales and Cumbria (the land between, say, the Ribble and Loch Lomond), did the British language, ancestor of modern Welsh, persist, in Cumbria perhaps until the twelfth century.

The early linguistic diversity of what is now Scotland does not reflect a simple ethnic division – Pict, Scot, Angle, Cumbrian. Each of the areas represented by these names must have been home to an earlier people and to later immigrants in unknown numbers. Wholesale expulsion of the former by the latter is improbable and was not the experience of other peoples, of Romanised Gauls under Franks and Visigoths, of Britons under Saxons and Jutes. Rather we should look for intermarriage and integration, at language-change as a sign of blending of peoples whose hierarchic social structures brought them closer than language divided them.

But the Anglian- and Cumbrian-speaking peoples south of the Forth were divided from the men of Alba to the north by geography, language and also by political organisation. Little is known of the kingdoms of the Cumbrians save that one was based upon the rock-fortress of Dumbarton at least (presumably) until its capture by Vikings in 872. If there were other kingdoms, they may have been absorbed into what seems to have been the successor-state to Dumbarton, the Strathclyde of some tenth-century accounts. Attacked by Danish settlers in Yorkshire and Norse settlers at Dublin, Strathclyde had an uncertain hold upon the lands around the Solway, and probably lost modern Cumberland to the advancing power of the Old English kings by the mid or late tenth century.

The uncertainty of that date, and indeed of the broad course of Cumbrian development, reflects the poverty of our sources for a crucial century – from the mid-ninth to the mid-tenth, the century of Scandinavian settlement in England, Ireland and Francia. True, we do know that there was a significant Danish settlement in Yorkshire in and after the reign of King Alfred, although scholars are still in debate about the numbers involved. The wars leading to that settlement destroyed the Anglian kingdom of Northumbria, leaving a rump between Forth and Tees, under a provincial headman, to find new allegiances. The kingdom of York, settled by Danes yet ruled by Norse from Dublin (a hybrid rather like the contemporaneous settlements which became Normandy), represents not merely the astonishing mobility of the Scandinavian peoples, and their hunger for land akin economically to that of their homeland, but also their failure to establish a stable successor state to the Anglian one they had destroyed.

But it also raises the intriguing question: why was there no significant Scandinavian inroad, still less settlement, in the relatively fertile eastern Lowlands of Scotland? The spread of Norse place-name elements outside the western seaboard and the far north of Scotland is restricted to the northern shores of the Solway and Dumfriesshire: perhaps suggesting that the silence of written sources about incursions into the east means that there were few or none.

By contrast the annals of the West Frankish kingdom dwell at length upon the terrible rapacity of the Northmen, and the terror which their arrival caused to the churches of the kingdom; we have graphic descriptions of the flight of monks with their holy relics from the exposed regions of the Seine and the Loire to safer eastern refuges. Much the same picture emerges from Irish annals and related literature. As places of sanctuary in war, churches had become safe-deposits for the silver and gold of laymen and ecclesiastics alike; beside their walls fairs were held which attracted large concourses of native peoples. To the Northmen these were standing invitations to plunder the church and sell the people into slavery. In the 860s and 870s the Irish Norse ravaged Alba for months at a time, though on one occasion their leader, Olaf, while transporting tribute, was killed by the Scottish king. About 903 the Norse were back, plundering Dunkeld 'and all Alba'; this time they seem to have wintered by the Tay for in the following year they were killed in Strathearn. To this invasion we could date the destruction of Forteviot as the royal centre and its replacement by Scone.

But this pattern is not found in eastern Scotland where there seem to be no Norse invasions across the North Sea. This suggests that not only were the precious objects rarer, but also that the ecclesiastical centres themselves were markedly fewer. We can certainly name some churches which can be traced back to the late tenth century and a few of these may be much older – St Andrews, Abernethy, Rosemarkie. But only Iona is known to have shared in the richness of culture of the Irish church, and that to an outstanding degree. From Iona the great Book of Kells and perhaps also the Book of Durrow reflect in parchment the glories of enamelled metalwork such as once must have adorned, say, the shrine of Columcille. Fragments of that do survive in Norway and Paris, evidence of the rapacity of the Norse who drove the monks of Iona to dispersion aound 800.

The east of Scotland displays degenerating lapidary statements of the same artistic themes, often at church sites – stones bearing the Cross, elaborately treated, and Pictish sculptures – and there is a tradition of native silver metalwork in chains and brooches, some of outstanding craftsmanship. There seems to have been much silver and even some gold in Alba about 850: if so, it was not attractive to Viking raiders. Either it was too dispersed or the defences of Alba deterred any bands which may have attacked on the east.

The question of Viking numbers is therefore as germane to the history of Scotland as to that of England or Ireland. The settlement of the Northern Isles was a stage on the way to raid and settle in the Hebrides and Ireland; when for a period in the late ninth century, Irish resistance deterred further attacks, the Vikings of the Hebrides carried out the settlement of the Faroes and Iceland, empty lands offering no resistance. It seems at least possible that the failure to attack eastern Scotland demonstrates the smallness of raiding and settling bands and the coherence of resistance in Alba.

For the men of Alba knew the obligation upon all to serve in war in defence of the province and kingdom, an ancient duty known to many peoples, Romans in the Republic, Franks and Anglo-Saxons. Such an obligation would undoubtedly become more active during the age of migrations and we have a list which shows some attempt to define it among the Scots of Dalriada as a duty based upon land held, and performed both by land and sea – a character which it retained on the western seaboard for almost a millennium. Among the men of Alba in the post-Viking age, however, it seems to become an instrument of aggression and of civil war.

Civil war is attested in the struggle for the throne, that symbol which was already at the ritual centre of Scone. Despite the long rule of two kings (Constantine II, 900–42, and Malcolm II, 1005–34), the annals of the quarter-millennium after 850 are the record of bloody struggles for the succession, with many kings dying in battle against their successors, and not a few battling with provincial rulers (*mormaer*, great steward) who, if they had won, might well have been successors. In both cases the resource which made these struggles possible was the right to call upon the host for either the realm or the province.

A mighty carved stele by the Kinloss road at Forres, laid out like a vertical strip cartoon, tells us what this could mean. (See page 8.) The long-eroded top seems to show nine horsemen; in the first distinct scene a helmeted figure in armour of quilted leather watches with a retinue of four, while eight spearmen engage in battle; in the next panel four men with spears stand beside a tower amid decapitated corpses and heads; they are above two fighting couples beside four men with swords or axes and shields coming to join the fray; below that six men on horseback flee from twelve infantry. The next scene has three fighting couples on each side of a canopy over dead bodies and severed heads, one of which is framed for emphasis, while at the bottom four men with shields now drive off fleeing infantry. This wonderful composition about a battle between the host of Quilted Coat and that of Framed Head was not composed from borrowed sketches or templates (as the Pictish hunting scenes probably were), but surely shows a real event, the matter of some Gaelic saga, now lost, in which four followers of Quilted Coat played a prominent part. That event is fortunately recorded for us: in 966, King Dubh 'was killed in Forres, and was hidden away under the bridge of Kinloss, but the sun did not appear as long as he was concealed there'. Men rode to battle but fought on foot; their arms were simple and their armour basic. If the tower is a church, then they ignored its sanctuary, spilled blood in a massacre and paid the price in more bloodshed, while the losing king, killed by his cousin's men, lay under the canopy of Kinloss bridge.

Kingship is on the other side of the stone, beneath a tall incised cross carved with elaborate interlace: a scarcely visible group of figures whose act seems to be the enthronement of a new king. Largely confined to one ruling kindred, the descendants of Alpin, whose son, Kenneth, was the first Scot to rule also over the Picts (842–58), kings might come from the sons and grandsons of a king, an openness of heritage found in England, in the Iberian kingdoms, widely, in fact, except in France where the Capetians ousted the Carolingians in the tenth century, and secured the uncontested successions of the eldest son as king by the practice of anticipatory election and consecration. In Scotland, however, close relatives were tempted to anticipate the death of a king by encompassing it; no satisfactory explanation of this has been offered by historians, partly because we have no contemporary literature describing any aspect of it, just a catalogue of violent successions like that of 966, unparallelled in England or Leon, but not in Ireland. Moreover, Alpin's descendants did not wholly monopolize kingship, for as early as 878 a Giric son of Dungal (a name unknown in the royal house) killed King Aed, and ruled for twelve years, subduing a territory which was probably Anglian Lothian, before falling victim to a successor of the house of Alpin (889). Probably within a century attempts had begun to smooth Giric's usurpation out of the record, rather than acknowledge him as an able and successful warrior who might have established his own kindred as the royal house.

Despite the return of the house of Alpin, Giric's reign marks a real break. Though the Scots had overcome the last Pictish kings in the 840s, our sources still call the kings between 842 and 878 kings 'of Picts'; after Giric's time his successors are kings 'of Alba', a new name for the kingdom, which can be shown to be the lands between the Forth on the south and the Spey on the north-west, linked by the 'spine of Alba', Drumalban, mountains which exclude from it the western seaboard, Lennox, Argyll and Moray, or at least the western part thereof. This was a shrunken land of the Picts, shorn of those peripheral regions settled by the Norse or dominated by the Irish and Orcadian Norse, and it certainly seems to formalize the loss of control over Argyll, whence the house of Alpin came. But otherwise it surely represents the replacement of a loose hegemony inherited from the Pictish kings by a tighter political unity, or at least pro-gramme of unity, with aggression and annexation to the south – to the Tweed by 1016, the Solway by 1018. The usurpation of Giric seems to mark the beginning of a kingdom of Alba, a Gaelic word which translates as 'Scotland'.

It has been suggested recently that Giric took his origins from a Dalriadic kindred of Loarn, and that they had established them-selves in a kingdom of Moray ('sea-province') existing alongside Alba for two hundred years. Certainly in the early eleventh century the provincial rulers of Moray claimed descent from fifth-century Loarn, and Irish writers sometimes called them kings; and certainly the most famous among them, Macbeth, was not descended from Alpin, and was able to become king of Alba by the defeat of the young Duncan I. But Shakespeare was neither the first nor the last to try to make sense of Macbeth and his times, and it is probably not greatly important whether Moray had 'kings', for it certainly had a dominant family, whose descent from Loarn might even be fact not fancy, and which enjoyed much independence of the kings of Alba.

Yet Macbeth's success came only after Malcolm II (1005–34) had eliminated rival kinsmen and passed the throne to his daughter's son. Duncan I was a military failure, heavily defeated at Durham, which must have destabilized his rule; but was his non-royal father another and decisive weakness, opening the way for Macbeth? Or were kinship ties through the mother acceptable, just as Macbeth's must have been accepted? Perhaps these questions are unanswerable, but they draw attention to the chequered history of the royal kin, and to the possibility that its edges were not clearly defined. By the end of the eleventh century that was undergoing change.

The complex circumstances in which Donald III ('Donalbane') seized the throne on the death of his brother, Malcolm III ('Canmore') in 1093 were the last assertion of the eligibility of all kin rather than of a single rightful heir (usually the eldest son), sign of a transformation to a rule of succession by a lineage, not a kin. This was no small matter, for kings were the visible living expression of loyalty and authority and of political unity. A kingdom derived its unity from its king, and continuity in kingship, peaceful succession to an inherited loyalty from subjects, built and strengthened the subjects' sense of common interest and common purpose in what by 1300 they would call usually their kingdom, but sometimes their land, country, nation. Chance played a part in this transformation: between 1097 and 1153 two kings had no son, and a third only one son, so there was no competing close kin.

Even so, the king of Scots had recourse to the Capetian model of designation in the father's lifetime; David I in 1152 (and probably about 1144) and William in 1201 had their heirs receive the homage of the magnates as an assurance of succession, ceremonies which reveal the weakness in Scottish kingship. For the church played no vital part in sanctifying the king. It was a curious consequence of the dilapidation of royal resources in ninth-century Francia that churchmen ceased to be royal poodles but, in at least some cases, made common cause with the king in defence of their authorities. Thus the great Hincmar of Reims was unable to save the Carolingians, but did contribute significantly to the development of a theory of divinely ordained monarchy, symbolised by ceremonies of coronation and unction, which made it difficult to destroy an anointed king or his anointed heir. The French king was poor in material resources but safe in God's armour.

In the same way the English monarchy owed much to Archbishop Dunstan and his conception of sacral kingship; it did not save Ethelred II or Harold II, but they fell to external foes, not to ambitious Englishmen. By contrast the Scottish bishops seemed unaware of the developing pretensions of leading sees elsewhere. Although blessed with relics of one of the apostles, the see of St Andrews and its bishops never appear as the foe of, or guide to, any king, do not assert their metropolitan status in any practical way, fail to assume or obtain the rank of archbishop, and play little, if any, role in the elevation of the king.

So kingship lacked the vital sanction of divine approval which could protect the individual king from the worst excesses of intra-familial rivalries. On the contrary, the episcopal churches of Scotland before 1100 seem to have been dependent upon rulers, royal and provincial, in a way which must have diminished their spiritual authority greatly. This, it seems, was one reason, and perhaps the principal one, why kingship in Alba between 850 and 1100 had such a turbulent history, a reason which cannot be laid at the door of Viking incursions, but must rather be seen as a consequence of the distant isolation of Scotland at that time from cultural and intellectual developments in western Europe. If we turn to native works of art from the eleventh century, we find only a tradition cut off from its Irish roots, ignorant of Byzantine, Carolingian or Anglo-Saxon inspiration, still copying antique models, though with deteriorating skills.

The second destination of military service identified above was aggression – the acquisition of booty and tribute from lands outside Alba. Kenneth, son of Alpin, warred as far as Dunbar, fortress of an Anglian headman, and Melrose, an Anglian monastery and presumably a deposit for lay wealth. Such activities are not well attested for his successors until the eleventh century, when each king seems to inaugurate his reign by an incursion into Northumberland, some-

times with an assault on Durham. Between these periods a significant change has taken place – the northern part of Northumbria,
between Tweed and Avon, ruled locally from Bamburgh, just south
of Tweed, passed under the rule of the king of Alba. Begun about
880, this change seems complete by the 970s and may have been so
as early as the beginning of the tenth century. Alba had become also
Scotland.

The western kingdom of Strathclyde remained in being, though its
bounds are a matter of conjecture; I believe that in the tenth century it lay between the Clyde and Solway, with Cumberland under the
distant authority of the ealdorman of Bamburgh. It is quite likely
that the King of Strathclyde acknowledged the lordship of the King
of Scotland when not forced to do homage (with the Scottish king)
to the King of England. Such loyalties were person-to-person and
lay lightly upon the consciences of those who promised them. In
1016, after a battle at Carham on the Tweed, the Northumbrian
ealdorman abandoned all claim to Lothian which lay north of
Tweed, and about the same time the kingship of Strathclyde too was
absorbed by the King of Scots.

Thus the Kingdom of Scotland or of the Scots came to reach
beyond the natural barrier of the Forth valley and to include lands
whose people spoke different languages. It happened because the
western territory was outflanked by the eastern advance, grasping
for the wealth of Northumbria from Tees to Forth, wealth which was
a modest spin-off from the developing economy of the English
realm, but which could not readily be defended by the English king
because of distance and the barrier of the kingdom of York.

But if the King of Scots could raid, take tribute, and even annex as
far as the Tweed, it is unlikely that his ambitions would stop there;
hence the eleventh-century raids into Northumberland. The Tyne,
the Tees or even the Humber, was as natural a frontier as the Tweed,
which represents the line of Scottish exhaustion, the line beyond
which resources would not maintain an occupation. We have not
often speculated why this should be so, and I can only suggest a possible reason. The critical century was the tenth, for thereafter the
English king was able to support the Northumbrian ealdorman, now
his subject. In the tenth century it would scarcely have been wise to
attempt the conquest of the men of Northumberland with armies of
their kinsmen, the men of Lothian. The Scottish king must have

drawn his invading armies from the old lands beyond the Forth. This factor of distance would make it very difficult, or, as it proved, impossible, to fix a permanent hold upon Northumberland by occupying its strongholds, by displacing its native lords, or by a combination of these.

The Kingdom of Scotland was created by an ambitious and able line of kings, often divided against one another and driven therefore to recruit support in their kingdom by offering the prospect of booty and tribute in neighbouring lands. The astonishing thing is that in diversifying the linguistic make-up of the kingdom, in multiplying its provinces by adding different peoples, the kings did not further destabilize their kingship, based as it was upon obsolescent sanctions. In part the reason must be the brevity of the land-frontier and absence of external foes who could inflict practical damage and loss of prestige.

There were foes other than the southern neighbour. When in 1098 the Norwegian king sought to bring to tribute, and some kind of obedience, the lands of the overseas Norse, by a great expedition to the Western seaboard, including Man and Anglesey, the Scottish king seems to have done little to resist him. Fearful, perhaps, of an army like that of Harold Hardrada which, supported by Malcolm III, invaded England in 1066, and which might inflict terrible damage unless bought off by a heap of silver, King Edgar (1097–1107) by treaty parted with the western fringe of, or beyond, his kingdom, a gesture which suggests that, when offered a trial of arms, the Scottish king preferred to lay down the time and conditions. He was none too sure of his own strength.

Already there were signs that the kings of Scotland on the periphery of Europe were aware of new influences. Perhaps the most striking of these was the visit of Macbeth to the threshold of the Apostle, the city of Rome. In making the pilgrimage and scattering money to the poor there, he showed the same devotion to the power of relics, the same remorse for his sins, as his near-contemporaries, the Emperor Conrad, Cnut King of England, Denmark and Norway, or Fulk Nerra, Count of Anjou. On his visit he would meet, or hear more of, Leo X, the reforming Pope who did much to restore the prestige of the Holy See and who sought a more canonical order in the Church. It may not be coincidence, therefore, that the death of Maelduin bishop of St Andrews in 1055 was followed by the early appointment of a successor. Macbeth did not keep the see vacant to draw its revenues. And finally, both he and his queen were patrons of the religious – as very few rulers of 850–1100 can be shown to have been. Macbeth is a dim figure, but when his shadow moves it is as the first King of a European Scotland.

Under his successor, Malcolm III, and the latter's queen, Margaret, these trends are noticeably stronger, and in the reigns of their sons, and particularly of the youngest, David I (1124–53), Scotland undoubtedly had a place in the comity of catholic realms. It restored a regular ecclesiastical organisation, received the new religious orders which revived the spiritual life of the Church, and accepted French secular culture which, allowing for local variants, dominated the ruling classes west of the Elbe – including much of Britain, where not only knighthood and chivalry, but also the French language and Romance literature inspired, even pervaded, the culture of the ruling élite.

This phenomenon bears the name of the Anglo-Norman age in Scotland's history, for it was marked by a sustained and dispersed immigration of men, mostly of French extraction though very rarely from France, from certain areas of England (Yorkshire and the north, the east Midlands and Dorset/Devon) first to southern Scotland and then, from about 1160, north of the Tay as far as Cromarty. These families have given us names from their French origins, such as Bruce, Hay, or Menzies, to become prominent in our history, but also names drawn from roots in England (Lindsay or Barclay) or from Wales (Wallace or Montgomery). For it has to be said that French influence was brief and probably confined to the most aristocratic of these families. Their dependents (and many of these came too) were, so far as we can tell, English-speaking and imbued with Romance culture as transmitted into English.

This new migration was not confined to the knights and barons whom the twelfth-century kings favoured with their patronage. It also extended to the ecclesiastical sphere where direct influence from France (e.g. from the monastery of Tiron) was short-lived. The new monastic orders sent English colonists to establish houses like the great Melrose or the modest Isle of May. A dynasty like that of Robert, bishop of St Andrews, whose family won many different offices in the Church, owed its opportunities to Robert's move as an Augustinian canon from Nostell in Yorkshire to the new priory at

Scone. Native names of bishops about 1120 – Cormac, Nectan – give way steadily to names from the Anglo-French repertoire – Robert, Turpin. Twelfth-century kings were the main, but by no means the only, benefactors of a church seeking a revived spiritual life and a new canonical order; the personnel for this change was initially drawn from outside the realm, especially from England.

And in the growth – we may not say renewal – of urban life too, men came to Scotland from the south to settle in the towns and to seek from the king the status of "burgh" which carried the same connotation of personal freedom and commercial privilege throughout north-western Europe. The best known of these immigrants came from Flanders, attracted, perhaps, by the particular favour of the king. But many moved north from English towns, perhaps to establish Scottish outlets for the family trading firm, perhaps to become master craftsmen who before had been only journeymen. This migration is poorly recorded, yet historians are agreed on its importance as bringing economic change and a further impetus to the spread of English speech in provinces north of Tay, formerly Gaelic.

In many respects these changes were similar to those taking place in the Slav country between Elbe and Oder. Here too native rulers sponsored the settlement of knights from the west, gave urban privileges and, using migration agencies, brought Germanic settlers into the new towns. Although the map bears witness in the Slavonic names of places to that major strand in the ethnic origin of the peoples of eastern Germany, the newcomers' language and culture prevailed and these lands became part of the German empire.

The comparison is instructive because in many respects eastern Germany did not develop an economy or society greatly different from those of its eastern neighbours. In other words these changes accompanied economic developments which, in broad terms, would have shown themselves irrespective of the immigration. So too in Scotland, the arrival of land-hungry younger sons of English barons and knights was an expression of economic need and a response to economic opportunity, the same need and opportunity which took Normans to carve out fiefs in Apulia or Palestine. For, in a period of climatic improvement, between about 1000 and 1300 AD, the European economy was in drastic flux from the late eleventh century, with demand for food rising as population increased. The consequent demand for land brought about colonial movements to many places, landless members of the land-owning class seeking more hectares and more labour to sustain their families in the dominant social position to which they were accustomed.   Evidence for increasing pressure upon the available land is found in the very earliest Scottish documents of the beginning of the twelfth century. Scotland could not be insulated from a movement which demanded increased production, and so created more wealth and a demand for more sophisticated goods, including manufactures. The changes are displayed in the structures which the landowners of the twelfth and thirteenth centuries put up for themselves, homes demonstrating a demand for security but compromising with the need for domestic comfort. Timber palisading gave way to masonry, curtain walls to halls and towers of increasing opulence. These things are a record of rising expectations and rising incomes.

Look at what just three castles can tell us of that wealth and of its limitations:

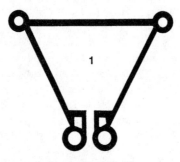

1. Caerlaverock Castle

At Caerlaverock by the Nith a large rectangular courtyard, surrounded by a ditch connected by a canal to the Solway was walled, perhaps by the Maxwell lord, around 1200–50; but it can scarcely have been finished when the walls were demolished and the masonry used by the same family to build a wholly new stone castle hardly a stone's throw away, on the plan of a triangle with round towers at the base corners and an entrance between twin towers at the apex. Again, the whole was surrounded by a deep ditch, manually dug.

2. Bothwell Castle as planned
in the thirteenth-century.
The walls represented by
the medium-thick line were
built later along the lines of
thirteenth-century plans,
and the enclosure was
completed by a wall along
the broken line.

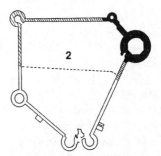

At Bothwell on the Clyde, where the estate fell to the Moray family by marriage in 1242, they built a massive round tower or donjon surrounded by a ditch with features strongly reminiscent of some at the castle of Coucy in northern France; Alexander II married Marie de Coucy in 1238. But before the end of the century something more ambitious was laid out, a pentagonal walled enclosure with round towers at three more corners and a gateway tower at the apex. It was never taken beyond the foundations (visible today), though a contracted form was built. Presumably the money ran out.

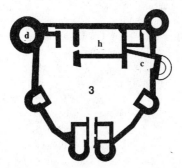

3. Kildrummy Castle. d: donjon. h: hall. c: chapel with foundations of unbuilt tower

Lastly, in Mar, a great round tower was similarly added to, in a plan which was also modified in that a chapel incorporated into the expanding structure, a vulnerable point, was to be masked by a great tower which was never built. The entrance tower was so sophisticated in plan that it has been claimed as the work of Edward I about 1300, despite the facts that his many castle accounts show no such expenditure, and that there is no stretch of time when he could have built it. The earl who built it wanted the latest and best, and thought – perhaps wrongly – that he could afford it.

Now the history of the twelfth and thirteenth centuries whether in the development of castles or of land tenure, monastic observances or kingship was undoubtedly influenced by the men who migrated from the south into Scotland. But if the forms of these changes were shaped by external influences, they were surely caused by economic (and consequent social) change, to which, indeed, we can also ascribe the migration itself. It would be wrong to say that the Anglo-Norman migration was not an important factor in the development of twelfth-century Scotland, for at the very least it diffused English speech and so made commerce and comity with English society readily possible. But it would be equally wrong to ascribe to Anglo-Norman migration alone the remarkable transformation of Scotland from a silent role outside the periphery of the European economy to an active producer of raw materials for export and an avid consumer of imports from many regions of western Europe. This is a change, it seems to me, which affects the whole of society and must also have its roots there.

Something did not change: land was the source of wealth, and those who owned it exploited their resource by the labours of others – a dependant peasantry whose obligations and servitudes varied in intensity over time and space, but who remained the creators of wealth. For this society had scarcely cracked the technical barrier to harnessing energy – the key to wealth creation – other than the muscle power of man or beast. In the fields the husbandman and cottar guided the plough and harrow, sowed by hand and reaped by sickle, hoed and sowed, drove, dipped and sheared sheep, cut and carried peats from the moss, and even humped coal from the holds of Newcastle ships up-country to the lord's hearth. They and their families sweated and ached to earn a share of what they produced, but the larger share undoubtedly went to the landowners, great and small, to whose discipline they were subject, and on whom they depended for the right to cultivate acres for themselves. They would be called to build and keep clear the lade taking water to turn the mill-wheel, and even to manhandle a new stone into the place of a worn or fractured one and be bound to pay the miller for having their grain turned by it into the meal which was their staple food, while the miller paid the lord each year for his lucrative monopoly.

The increasing number of mills is an important indication of expanding production in these centuries; but the sophistication of their machinery, for both wind and water power were used, was also a response to the need to feed a rising population. For here, and here only, man had found ways of using the energy of natural forces.

The GNP, we could say, was increasing: those who had wealth must protect it. Among consumers of wealth, the landed class, therefore, customary protection of landownership by the oral testimony of neighbours ceased to be adequate in the twelfth century and was supplemented, then replaced, by written record. The growing emphasis upon warrandice (guarantee) of tenure on parchment, demanded by tenant or landlord, shows the nature of the fief or feu: it is property, an asset. That it is held for homage and fealty seems to mean little – a man is willing to take from two, three, even ten lords, those bonds which imply or state adherence to only one lord; vassalage had become a form only, the philosopher's accident; the substance was the feu. Feudal custom was early mercantile law.

Government might tinker with the rules governing the exploitation of this asset, but neither then nor now could it buck the great movements of economic and social change. Nor did it wish to do so, for as the greatest of all individual landowners, the king too benefited from the rising profitability of land, the expanding horizons of commerce. First through the towns, then from his estates also, he drew income in cash. With patronage and liquid wealth he was able to command widespread allegiance, willing obedience, and, if necessary, physical support against any foe. The internal challenges to twelfth-century kings were seen off by them with an ease which their tenth- and eleventh-century predecessors would have envied.

It was the enormously increased resources provided by the commercial economy of the twelfth and thirteenth centuries which enabled kings from David I to Alexander III to rule, overwhelmingly peaceably. They built no ostentatious towers like London or Dover, or Bothwell and Kildrummy, but only the modest structures such as those lost in brambles and trees at Kincardine and Kinclaven. Relatively free of foreign commitments, they had little need to tax or tallage, and resentment at their occasional mistakes was modest and fleeting. Perhaps as much from necessity as inclination, they consulted leading magnates, and in politics steadily built up a habit of command and obedience through all social ranks. Thus the difference between their subjects and those of, say, the king of England, was appreciated ever more clearly. Asked to define 'Scotland', a thirteenth-century commentator would have replied 'the lands of those who are *fideles*, sworn subjects, of the King of Scots'. That these were of varying ethnic origin and spoke different tongues, did not, or at least should not, signify; their common allegiance to one king made the land a kingdom and them a community. It was as kingdom and then as community, that Scotland was put together.

Yet there was a real social and linguistic divide within the kingdom, real geographical limits to the community which did not, in fact, comprehend all those who nominally accepted the king. These limits corresponded, generally, to the boundaries of the predominantly agrarian economy. In Highland regions where the economy was largely pastoral the cattle of Argyll, sold at the fairs of Glasgow, Stirling or Lanark, paid for Argyll castles built by chieftains with little or no Anglo-Norman blood. But no towns grew within the region, no burghal privileges were granted beyond Dumbarton or Dingwall, Lowland centres to which the men of the *Gaidhealtachd* must come for commerce.

Thus the spread of the English language was halted at the limits of commerce and manufacture, for although the wealth earned by pastoral activity did find its way home, the land was not suited to feed greater numbers of people by more intensive growing of cereals; the balance of pastoral and agrarian activity did not greatly change, and it was in the latter that the potential of major population-rise lay. The Highlands were affected by the boom of the twelfth century, but in a modest expansion of production which did not attract lively mercantile activity. A few Anglophone knights or barons were attracted to take land in the broader straths of e.g. Speyside or Glassary, but the Highland economy offered limited opportunities for expansion and grew relatively slowly. Highland society coped with change while maintaining its own language and in some respects its traditional culture.

But this had become the culture, probably, of a minority in Scotland. If we knew more of Highland society we might find that it was less hierarchical, less exploitative, had fewer extremes of wealth, than the manorialised economy of Lowland regions; but differences were surprisingly well under control by the thirteenth century, perhaps because some Highland chiefs sought to ape Lowland barons. Both contributed to the evolution of a socially and politically peaceful realm. But the difference was there and was to affect the history of the kingdom for many centuries to come.

The Middle Ages: the Defence of Independence

ALEXANDER GRANT

Reader in History, Lancaster University

THE MOST OBVIOUS REASON WHY Scottish history matters is that otherwise the concept of 'a Scot' is meaningless. Without a past, a people had neither a present nor a future; this applies as much to those who consider themselves Scots (of whatever political persuasion) as to the other peoples of the world. It is, in fact, its history which defines a people, by demonstrating its distinctiveness. Thus the events of Scotland's past have made the Scots into what they are today. But since no people exists in a vacuum, one people's history inevitably impinges upon the histories of others. With regard to Scotland, that is particularly true of its effects on England; indeed English and especially British history cannot be studied properly without paying full attention to Scotland. The Scots, moreover, being one of the family of West European peoples, played their part in, and so have their contribution to make to, the wider field of European history.

The vital importance of history is something that was appreciated – perhaps for the first time – in the middle ages. From the thirteenth to the fifteenth centuries the histories of the various European countries were written down, as part of the process of legitimising and consolidating their existence. In Scotland, the most important examples are the *Chronicle of the Scottish People*, by John Fordun (1380s), the *Orygynale Cronikil* (i.e. from the origins of the world), by Andrew Wyntoun (1410s), and the *Scotichronicon* (*Scottish Chronicle*), by Walter Bower (1440s). They were produced following the great Anglo-Scottish wars of the late thirteenth and early fourteenth centuries, and were written to demonstrate, by means of its history, that Scotland was a proper, independent state, on a par with any other in Europe. Their ethos is perfectly summed up in Bower's concluding words: 'O Christ, he is not a Scot who is not pleased with this book'. Nowadays, Bower is perhaps turning in his grave.

Be that as it may, Fordun, Wyntoun and Bower established a narrative framework for Scotland's mediaeval history that survived for centuries. Theirs was an impressive achievement, which served the Scottish people well. In the nineteenth century, however, when 'modern' historical methods moved away from chronicle-based narratives towards record-based analyses, interpretations of mediaeval Scotland did not follow suit. That was partly because nineteenth-century historians concentrated on the great 'nation states' – France, Germany and Britain (in effect England) – with smaller countries being deemed less deserving of study, or even unworthy of having a history and hence of any claims to separate existence. (German scholars dismissed Danish history in that way.) Partly, too, religious antagonisms inside Scotland meant that those who did study Scottish history tended not to be objective about the pre-Reformation era. But the chief reason is that for English-speaking historians of the time the most important advances were in mediaeval England's constitutional and legal history. England's past was depicted as a sequence of constitutional struggles along the road to parliamentary democracy, which were readily studied thanks to an abundance of surviving records. Nowadays it is realised that the struggles were personal as much as constitutional, that copious records indicate bureaucratic inertia as much as good governance, and that Scotland's sparser records and absence of constitutional conflict simply reflect interesting differences in its government and political society. But at the time when 'modern' historical study was developing in Britain, Scottish mediaeval history was seen as inferior, as a much less valid subject. The consequences of that are still with us today, especially in the world outside the universities.

So far as current academic history is concerned, however, the situation has changed dramatically. The emphasis on mediaeval England's constitution and law has gone; English historians are now much more concerned with what actually happened and with how things actually worked in practice. Such an approach is much the same as that adopted by Scottish mediaeval historians since the 1950s. And nowadays English historians fully accept the validity, significance and interest of mediaeval Scottish history – and Welsh and Irish history likewise; the point applies to all three 'Celtic' countries. There is even a growing sense that in some respects the most constructive and stimulating work is being done by Welsh,

Irish and Scottish historians. The admirable new survey by an Irish historian, Dr Robin Frame, *The Political Development of the British Isles, 1100–1400* (Oxford, Opus paperback, 1990), which replaces the traditional Anglocentric viewpoint with a genuine British perspective treating Wales, Ireland and Scotland on a par with England, is an excellent case in point.

Thus Scottish mediaeval history has come to be a much more acceptable subject for study than it has been for generations. That applies throughout the historical spectrum. There is, for instance, major work on administrative, religious, intellectual, social, and economic subjects, which clearly demonstrates their historical importance in both a Scottish and a wider context, their vital contributions towards creating the Scottish people, and their present-day relevance. But above all, especially for general readers and school students, it is political history that matters most from Scotland's mediaeval past – as is strikingly indicated by the tee-shirt slogan *'1314 Bannockburn: 1307 Murrayfield'* which was produced after Scotland won a famous rugby victory over England by 13 points to 7 at Murrayfield, Edinburgh, in 1990.

Looking broadly at mediaeval Scotland's political history, the most interesting general point seems to be, remarkably, the importance of what did *not* happen. Mediaeval Scotland was not conquered either by the Normans after 1066 or by Edward I and his successors after 1296; and it did *not* suffer nearly as many internal wars and violent power struggles as other mediaeval countries, especially England. The rest of this chapter will discuss why that was so. In the process, some of the main reasons why Scottish mediaeval history should matter in Scottish, British and European contexts will, it is hoped, be clearly illuminated.

To begin with, why was there no Norman Conquest of Scotland – neither sudden, as in England, nor piecemeal, as in Wales and Ireland? The answer probably lies in the fact that in Britain the centuries before 1066 witnessed the emergence of not one but two relatively unified kingdoms: in the south, Anglo-Saxon England, and in the north a Gaelic, or Anglo-Gaelic, Scotland which was, recent work has stressed, probably almost as powerful. The pre-1066 development of Scotland is vital. It meant that after 1066, the kingdom was not open to the kind of piecemeal conquest which individual Norman barons carried out in Wales, and while (like England) it might have succumbed to a full-scale Norman invasion, the Norman kings of England were too busy with their continental concerns to have the time or resources for any lengthy campaigns north of the Border. Instead, Anglo-Scottish relations after 1066 were essentially fairly good; the north-south division of the British mainland continued; and the kingdoms of England and Scotland developed side by side.

They also developed in much the same way, because David I (1124–53) and his successors deliberately copied English models, for instance restructuring their administration along Anglo-Norman lines. The effect was to turn Scotland into a fairly typical west European kingdom (albeit one in which there was also much continuity with the Gaelic past: this is one of the most fascinating aspects of current work on mediaeval Scotland). A major part of the process was the kings' invitation of many Anglo-Normans into Scotland, so that by the end of the twelfth century the Scottish nobility and Church had been extensively Normanised. It might therefore seem irrelevant that there was no Norman Conquest of Scotland. But had that happened, British history would have been very different, for Scotland would have been absorbed into England. Also, the Normanisation of Scotland did not cause any wholesale displacement of native landowners. Instead, a hybrid Scoto-Norman landowning society evolved peacefully, with all its members, whatever their origins, owing allegiance to the king of Scots. The contrast with the fates of the Saxons in England, the Welsh in Wales and the Irish in Ireland is obvious: so too is the significance of what happened in Scotland, for Scottish, British and European history alike.

Furthermore, in Scotland the Normans' well-nigh invincible military machinery, based on knights and castles, was used for, not against, the Scottish crown. That meant that the twelfth- and thirteenth-century Scottish kings, unlike their predecessors, could always defeat challenges by rival claimants to the throne. And the military power at the kings' disposal enabled royal authority to be extended into the kingdom's periphery: to Galloway; to Moray and beyond; and, in the mid-thirteenth century, to the north-western seaboard, culminating in the cession of the Western Isles by the king of Norway in 1266. This epitomises the steady strengthening of Scottish kingship during the twelfth and thirteenth centuries – a strengthening based on the co-operation of Crown and Normanised aristocracy, which contrasts strikingly both with the process of "predatory" centralisation (as Professor Southern has described it) found in Norman and Plantagenet England and with the conflicts which resulted there.

The successful Scottish Crown was soon, however, to face its greatest challenge. During the thirteenth century the focus of English foreign policy shifted from France to Britain. In the 1280s Edward I conquered the last independent part of Wales, and when the sudden death of Alexander III in 1286 brought the direct line of Scottish kings to an end, he turned his attention to Scotland. The result, ultimately, was the Wars of Independence (1296–1357), in which Edward I, Edward II, and Edward III all expended huge amounts of money and resources in attempting to conquer Scotland. As G. L. Harriss's major work, *Crown, Parliament and Public Finance in England to 1360* (Oxford U.P., 1975), demonstrates, the strains imposed by the war in Scotland are fundamentally important for the history of the English Crown and constitution. But in Scotland, despite their efforts, the three Edwards all failed. Although there were several crushing English victories in battle, Scottish resistance never died out altogether, and in the long run Scotland's independence was triumphantly maintained. The Scots, in fact, won their mediaeval wars with England; this is arguably the most important single point about mediaeval British history.

Why were the Scots, unlike the Welsh, able to avoid English conquest? Among many factors, the chief is probably that Edward I's Anglocentric viewpoint misled him (and many subsequent historians) into thinking that his tasks in Wales and in Scotland were the same. In fact, as adopting a British viewpoint makes clear, they were very different. Most of Wales had already been conquered by Anglo-Norman barons; Edward I had only the north-west to subdue, and in doing so he completed the final stage of the Normanisation of Wales. The Scottish parallel is the completion of the Normanisation of Scotland, when the royal authority reached the north-west in the 1260s. Thus in a British context, Edward I was attempting something completely new in Scotland: attacking another Normanised kingdom, where the Normanised nobility did not support him, as the Anglo-Norman barons in Wales had done, but instead led the Scottish resistance.

This was crucial. In Wales, Edward I used the Anglo-Norman baronage to consolidate his conquest; they already controlled most of the country, and were given much of the newly-conquered land. But how could Edward consolidate his Scottish victories? Scotland's Normanised landowners were not his men, unlike their counterparts in Wales. So he either had to expropriate them – which was virtually impossible – or hope to persuade or force them to transfer their allegiance from the Scottish to the English Crown. At times that did seem feasible, but in the long run the Scottish élites could neither be trusted nor forced to collaborate permanently. There is no simple explanation for this; few Scottish nobles showed absolute consistency. But two things probably ensured that enough Scots fought for enough time to maintain the cause of independence.

One is ideological. During the twelfth and thirteenth centuries the political community, although Normanised, acquired a distinct sense of Scottishness. This usually centred on the king, but the abstract concept of the kingdom also developed. After Alexander III's death, when the kingdom was ruled by 'Guardians', their great seal showed not the usual royal figures but the lion rampant and St Andrew, with the legends, 'The Seal of Scotland appointed for the government of the kingdom' and 'Andrew be leader of the Scots, your fellow countrymen'. In 1304, the defenders of Stirling Castle said they held it 'of the Lion'. Here we have one of the earliest and most striking examples of the appearance of the abstract concept of the state in mediaeval European history. In Scotland, it gave an essential stimulus and rallying-point for those brave or recalcitrant enough to resist English might; and in 1320 it reached its full development in the Declaration of Arbroath, which stated that any Scottish king who submitted to the English would be deposed by the Scottish community. This is one of the clearest and most dramatic statements of 'popular' sovereignty to be expressed in the mediaeval world – putting the Declaration on a par with Magna Carta.

Secondly, there is the military factor. After Scotland's mounted knights had been routed by Edward I in 1296, resistance leaders worked out new methods of waging war, using foot-soldiers armed with long pikes and axes. Mediaeval infantry usually fled when charged by cavalry, but William Wallace and Robert Bruce (King Robert I) solved the problem by organising their men into massed formations ('schiltroms'), and fighting on the defensive on well-chosen ground;

that is how Robert I's army won the battle of Bannockburn. Also, Robert ordered that castles recaptured from the English should be demolished or slighted. This denied the English any bases for garrisons, and meant that subsequent warfare consisted chiefly of cross-Border raids – in which Robert I perfected the technique of making rapid hard-hitting strikes. The English could not win this kind of warfare. The actual fighting was done by ordinary Scotsmen; most of the pikemen came from the substantial peasantry, whose level of commitment to the independence cause was remarkably high. But the organisation and leadership came from the Normanised Scottish landowners. Norman military success had been based on these qualities as well as on armoured cavalry; now they were vital in countering the armies of English knights. There is a most significant contrast here with the Welsh and the Irish, who never found the way to defeat the English in warfare. It was the Normanised Scottish landowners, forming the 'officer corps' of Scotland's armies, who achieved that crucial breakthrough.

The importance of this extends far beyond Scotland. The battles of Bannockburn (1314), Courtrai (Flemings against French, 1302) and Morgarten (Swiss against Austrians, 1315) make up a trio of victories by infantry over the previously dominant mounted knights. Together they reflect a general shift away from cavalry – and since the knight's military pre-eminence was what lay behind feudal society, they also indicate a major social change. And Bannockburn is probably the most significant of the battles, because the English, unlike the French and Austrians, learned from their enemy. By the 1330s they were defeating defensive Scottish pikemen not with cavalry but with a combination of archers and dismounted men-at-arms. These tactics were subsequently used to devastating effect by Edward III and his successors in France. Similarly, Edward's strategy of fast-moving raids to 'blitz' French territory derived from the Scots raids on northern England. The English successes in the Hundred Years' War with France are of immense significance in British and European history; they would not have happened but for the lessons learned in Scotland.

One other important aspect of the Wars of Independence must be mentioned. Whereas in England and on the Continent late-mediaeval warfare led to the development of paid, contract armies, the Scottish forces consisted of 'freedom fighters', who were simply raised according to the fundamental obligation to defend the homeland, and who fought without pay. The Scottish military machine was a unique blend of new military techniques and old methods of recruitment; the latter were obsolescent elsewhere, but in Scotland there was no need to change them, since they had successfully provided the manpower for Robert I's triumphs.

Now, in mediaeval England the constant demands of the Crown for taxation and resources to sustain foreign warfare caused much of the political conflict and most of the constitutional development from Magna Carta onward: English parliamentary democracy grew on the back of the mediaeval Crown's aggressive imperialism! In Scotland, on the other hand, fiscal pressure was much lighter, and so Scotland's constitutional and institutional history was very different. Consider the Parliament of Scotland. As in England, it was the supreme legislative, judicial, fiscal and administrative body, the forum where king and political community met to deal with whatever the kingdom's interests required. And, on occasions, it opposed Scottish kings on exactly the same grounds as its English counterpart. But, because the Scottish Crown's fiscal demands were so much less, these occasions were infrequent. Instead, the operations of the Scots Parliament are characterised by co-operation between Crown and political community – while the main emphasis of mediaeval Scottish constitutional history was on the fundamental principle of Scotland's independence. In both England and Scotland, in fact, parliamentary development was largely consequential on the English king's foreign warfare. (Interestingly, it has recently been shown that in negotiations during the late 1280s the Scots raised exactly the same objections to Edward I's kingship as his domestic opposition did a decade later.)

The relative lack of fiscal demands by the mediaeval Scottish Crown, and its consequently low financial turnover, is often seen as reflecting royal weakness. The result certainly was that financial and other administrative institutions did not develop so far as in England. On the other hand, that the Scottish kings could raise armies without having to pay them could well be seen as indicating the strength of the Crown's position. In fact, notions of strength or weakness are misleading when discussing mediaeval kingship. In England, the apparent strength of the English Crown, when applied heedlessly, often led to political crises, for example over recruitment, military provisioning and taxation. It was also a serious problem with respect to justice and administration, especially in the localities; the manipulation of these for partisan ends was unfortunately frequent, and is a major underlying cause of the Wars of the Roses. This point about English history is strongly highlighted by comparisons with Scotland. There, because the twelfth- and thirteenth-century kings generally had good relations with their nobles which were not soured then or later by fiscal pressure, the Crown both before and after the Wars of Independence was content to let the nobility look after local justice and administration. This no doubt caused problems in individual cases, but did not give much opportunity for those in power at the centre to favour their supporters in the localities. Abuse of patronage, and the widespread antagonism to the Crown which that usually stimulated, were therefore much rarer phenomena in Scotland which experienced nothing like the Wars of the Roses. In many ways, indeed, mediaeval England's domestic political history illustrates the dangers of taking centralisation to excess, while mediaeval Scotland's demonstrates the advantages of tolerating relative local autonomy.

It does not follow that in late mediaeval Scotland the localities were independent of the centre. The extension of supervisory (if not interventionist) royal authority to the periphery of the kingdom during the twelfth and thirteenth centuries established a system of governmental relationships which continued after the Wars of Independence – wars which had greatly intensified the concept of a collective Scottish political community under the Crown, in which internal conflicts had to be avoided, lest they gave the English an opportunity to attack. As a result, individual opponents of the government generally found little support, and political disputes mostly ended in compromise; there were few successful rebellions against a Scottish king in the fourteenth and fifteenth centuries. Much more typical was the fate of the two great noble families, the Douglases (earls of Douglas) and the MacDonalds (Lords of the Isles and Earls of Ross). Both were headed in the mid-fifteenth century by magnates who flagrantly disregarded Crown superiority; both were crushed and their estates forfeited, the Douglases in sudden royal action during the 1450s, the MacDonalds more slowly but nonetheless decisively in the 1470s and 1490s. In each case this was achieved by kings acting in conjunction with the greater part of the political community. That combination was the norm in mediaeval Scottish politics; it meant that in domestic affairs, just as in external, the Scots Crown was highly effective.

The forfeiture of the MacDonald Lords of the Isles raises a final point. Crown–MacDonald tension had been fairly constant in the fourteenth and fifteenth centuries because the MacDonald Lords never really fitted into the political community like the other magnates. Generally, however, the quarrels were over MacDonald expansion eastwards, up and across the Great Glen, rather than over their west-coast power, and despite quarrels, rebellions and even pitched battles it was not until the 1490s that the king destroyed their position in the West. In the sixteenth century this resulted in a power vacuum and the severe upheavals which made the region appear ungovernable. The contrast with the fourteenth and fifteenth centuries, when the MacDonald might kept the West relatively peaceful (at least internally), once more emphasises the importance of strong local lordship in mediaeval Scotland. And although the Lords of the Isles caused problems for the Scottish Crown outside the Lordship, their forfeiture in the sixteenth century produced a much more serious situation.

Moreover, the Crown–MacDonald conflicts of the fourteenth and fifteenth centuries do not typify relations between the Gaelic North and West and the rest of the kingdom. Admittedly there was a growing awareness of Highland–Lowland divisions, famously articulated by John Fordun in the 1370s. But while Fordun contrasted savage Highlanders with civilized Lowlanders, he carefully stressed that 'the Highlanders are, however, faithful and obedient to their king and country, and easily made to submit to law, if properly governed'. That is borne out by the history of most Highland families, including, of course, the Campbells of Argyll, whose later vilification by MacDonald propagandists obscures the fact that they acted for the Crown (and naturally themselves) to govern their region in much the same way as most other Scottish regional magnates. And Fordun also took great pains to emphasize that despite their ethnic and linguistic differences, both Lowlanders and Highlanders belonged to the same Scottish nation, which he distinguished carefully from the English. In so arguing, Fordun contradicted contemporary theories which equated nations with single ethnic races and languages; but he accurately reflected the situation existing within

Scotland. It was a hybrid kingdom, based on co-operation between among its racial and linguistic groups.

As the leading Welsh historian Professor R R Davies has commented, the achievement of the Scottish kings in keeping ultimate authority over this hybrid kingdom was very remarkable indeed: 'There are surely questions to be pondered here, and not just by Scottish historians' (*The British Isles, 1100–1500* [Edinburgh, John Donald, 1988], p.51). Whatever the answers, hybridity was a feature of the kingdom of the Scots even during its initial consolidation; it was reinforced with the introduction of Norman lords and lordships in the twelfth century; and it continued throughout the central and later middle ages. The point is perfectly epitomised in the career of Colin Campbell of Lochawe, MacCailein Mór, Chief of Clan Campbell, first earl of Argyll (1457), Master of the Royal Household (1464), and Chancellor of Scotland (1483).

The kings themselves reflect this continuing hybridity. They may have been called Bruce or Stewart in the later middle ages, and have been for the most part characteristic late mediaeval monarchs, but (like our present queen) they were the direct successors of what the Declaration of Arbroath called 'one hundred and thirteen kings of their own royal stock . . . , the line unbroken by a single foreigner'. It was, of course, a Gaelic royal stock. For all the Normanisation of families, government, institutions and landholding, the Crown's position and power derived ultimately from the Gaelic dynasty of kings. Mediaeval Scotland thus exhibits a unique combination of Gaelic and Anglo-Norman kingship, which compares and contrasts in a fascinating way with the other countries of western Europe. It is the realization of this point that is currently making Scottish mediaeval history so interesting. In addition, as seen throughout this essay, the combination of the Gaelic, the Anglian and the Norman influences in Scotland's development helped to make it one of the great success stories of the European middle ages. And that is something of which all who consider themselves Scots should be both aware and proud.

The Age of Renaissance and Reformation

MICHAEL LYNCH

Professor of Scottish History, Edinburgh University

THE SIXTEENTH CENTURY in Scotland is usually thought of as the century of John Knox and Mary, Queen of Scots. But the contest between them was not simply that of Protestant preacher versus Catholic queen. Each had had formative years on the continent of Europe: Knox had been in France, Frankfurt and Geneva as well as England in the 1550s; Mary had been brought up at the glittering Valois court of Henri II, had seen at first hand the dangers of the growth of militant Calvinism and had left France on the eve of the unsuccessful attempt of her uncle, the Cardinal of Lorraine, to find a Gallican solution to the religious problem by reconciling Catholics and moderate Lutherans and isolating the Calvinist extremists. Each was aware that both Protestant ideas and the intellectual alternatives to them had, in the generation since 1525, flowed along the natural conduits which linked Scotland with Europe – the trade routes, especially with the Netherlands, France and the Baltic, and the paths trodden by countless scholars between the Scottish universities and those in the Low Countries and France. Knox and Mary used the new weapons available to the sixteenth century – the printing press and the iconography of kingship. The Church of the 'trumpeter of God' relied on printed catechisms, bibles and psalm books as a means of mass evangelisation as well as on the pulpit. Mary's court, as well as offering the Mass and a rejuvenated Catholicism within the privileged confines of the Queen's household, would provide a Mecca for a renewal of both the cult of honour and literary patronage; they were two strands of a concerted assault on the minds of her great subjects. The struggle between Calvinist firebrand and Catholic monarch was about different aspects of the Renaissance as well as about rival versions of Reformation.

Part of the official entry into her capital which greeted Mary when she returned to Scotland in 1561 was a Protestant demonstration;

she was presented with a psalm book and subjected to a very Protestant homily.   That reception, like the famous interviews between her and Knox, oversimplified the issues at stake during her personal reign.   There was a more elaborate and more intriguing welcome staged for Charles I on his first visit to his Scottish kingdom in 1633.   A huge timber Parnassus was built in the middle of the High Street, beside the Salt Tron (some yards to the west of where the Tron Church would be constructed after 1636).   On it, amidst a double-topped mountain 'stopit full with books', were displayed representations of the 'ancient worthies of Scotland for learning', mostly drawn from the century before 1560.   They included Duns Scotus, Scotland's most celebrated academic philosopher; Robert Henryson, schoolmaster and the greatest poet of the age of James IV; William Elphinstone, a rector of Glasgow University, later bishop of Aberdeen and founder of King's College, Aberdeen, the third of Scotland's universities;   Hector Boece, chronicler and the first rector of Aberdeen's new university; John Mair (or Major), logician and author of a *History of Greater Britain* (1525), and a teacher at Glasgow and Paris before he became principal of St Leonard's College at St. Andrews; Gavin Douglas, royal tutor, bishop of Dunkeld, author of the 'Palace of Honour' and translator of Virgil's *Aeneid*; Sir David Lindsay, herald, tutor to James V, poet and playwright, whose most famous work, 'The Satire of the Three Estates', had first been performed at Edinburgh in 1539;   and George Buchanan, another principal of St Leonard's, one of the most famous humanists of the sixteenth century, Latin court poet to Mary, Queen of Scots, and tutor to her son James VI, author of the most influential history of Scotland, first published in 1582, as well as moderator of the General Assembly of 1567, when Mary, Queen of Scots was deposed.   From out of the mountain came the Muses, boys (probably from the High School) who sang to the King, and Apollo, who presented him with a book to emphasise that not only had Charles inherited the kingdoms of Scotland and England but also Apollo's kingdom of the arts.

The Parnassus of 1633 clearly showed what mattered in Scottish history then.   Already evident was the concern for learning which has marked so much of Scotland's history.   Amongst the 'worthies' were five academics and a schoolmaster.   All of Scotland's first three universities were represented and the Parnassus had been organised by John Adamson, principal of the fourth – the Edinburgh toun college, founded in 1583. Typically, a number of the schoolmen represented – most notably Mair and Boece – had pursued an academic career in the leading universities on the continent before returning to their native land. The Church and learning had formed the main channels through which Scotland's links with Europe – in both directions – had run. In 1560 or 1638 as much as in 1450, students went abroad to pursue a second degree: in the fifteenth and early sixteenth centuries, their most usual destinations were the universities of Louvain and Cologne; Paris was the favourite resort of promising Scots scholars for the two generations either side of the Reformation of 1560; by the 1580s the Calvinist University of Heidelberg and the Huguenot *académies* had taken over from Beza's Geneva; and by 1625 Leiden in the Netherlands had become a Mecca for the two rising professions, the ministry and the law.

Equally characteristic was Elphinstone's justification of King's College – 'pro patria'. Both before and after the Reformation of 1560, a virtual national curriculum, overseen by the Church, had operated in the country's grammar schools. Most pre-Reformation schoolmasters were clerics or chaplains and the *First Book of Discipline* of 1560–1, the blueprint for a godly Reformation, had more to say about education than any other single topic. Part of its text had, ironically, been borrowed from the decrees of the first session of the Catholic Council of Trent, for a national system of schooling was part of a broad humanist concern which marked the middle decades of the sixteenth century throughout much of Western Europe. Learning was a bridge across the troubled waters of the Reformation.

The Parnassus also celebrated three of Scotland's most recent historians – Boece, Mair and Buchanan. Another part of the 1633 formal entry into Charles I's was an 'Arch of Genealogy', the work of the well-known painter George Jamesone, who devised portraits of 107 kings of Scots stretching back to Fergus mac Erc (who materialised to present the King with his genealogy) and beyond, into the mists and whimsy of antiquity. Mair, a proponent of Union between Scotland and England (though on more equitable terms than those which emerged after the 1603 Union of the Crowns), was Scotland's first serious historian. Buchanan, prophet of the Scottish Revolution which would within five years of 1633 challenge Charles I's rule, was its best known; the Scots, it was said, went to war against Charles I in 1639 with the Geneva Bible in one saddlebag and Buchanan's *History* in the other.   The *History*, written in elegant Latin, embellishing the long line of legendary (and mostly apocryphal) kings of Scots charted by Boece, was published and republished, both on Scotland and on the continent of Europe, in countless editions in the century after his death.   Boece had been a pensioner of James V. Buchanan's work, written to justify the deposing of Queen Mary in 1567, would by contrast be censored, banned and excoriated by proponents of royalism throughout the seventeenth century; in 1683, for example, at the height of the Tory reaction of the 1680s, his works were publicly burned along with those of Milton, Hobbes and the Huguenot pamphleteer Languet – a remarkable Whig 'gang of four'.   The history of Scotland reached an international audience in the century after 1580: Buchanan's *History* had been commissioned by the 'Sidney circle', a group of men of letters headed by the Elizabethan soldier-poet, Sir Philip Sidney, and including Edmund Spenser, author of the epic *Faerie Queen* and a history of Ireland. At home, it became the Latin primer of the universities and formed the mainspring for the Scots' own view of themselves well into the early part of the eighteenth century.

In 1507, Scotland acquired its first printing press.   The licence granted to the two printers, Chepman and Myllar, specified 'bukis of our lawis, actis of parliament, chroniclis, mes bukis'. Print was a new means of promoting government, the image of kingship and the place of the Church. In the reign of James VI, the official uses to which printed books were put were much the same as in the reign of James IV: the most frequently printed works were individual Acts of Parliament and the largest print runs were reserved for the *Psalms* and catechisms, the two chief weapons in the armoury of the reformed Church. In the inventory of Henry Charteris, an Edinburgh bookseller who died in 1599, there were listed over 3,300 psalm books of various sorts and 5,400 copies of Calvin's *Smaller Catechism*, in its simple question and answer format which cost only 2d and was designed for use in the 'English' or vernacular schools, where children up to the age of eight were taught.

There were, however, other best-sellers of the age of James VI – and the worthies on the Parnassus were well represented amongst them. The works of Sir David Lindsay, chief poet at the court of James V, had been reprinted by Charteris in 1568 and in 1599 he had 788 copies of it in stock. Also in Charteris's stock were 554 copies of the *Testament of Cresseid,* the most popular of the works of Robert Henryson. It had been Charteris who had led the way in making available to a new reading public both the literary masterpieces of Middle Scots and the formative histories of late mediaeval Scotland: he had in 1570 commissioned an edition of Blind Harry's late fifteenth-century epic, *The Wallace,* and in the following year John Barbour's late fourteenth-century heroic romance, *The Brus.*

The bulk of the likely reading public for such works were the rising 'middling sort' – lairds, feuars, merchants and lawyers. Charteris's edition of Lindsay's works was priced at 8s, but he also sold cheaper copies of individual works, such as a 4d edition of Henryson's *Cresseid,* which had a wider appeal. By 1600, there were clear signs of the emergence of a new self-confident literary society, independent of both the royal court and the noble household, and with its own tastes and demands. The Scottish Renaissance, usually associated with the courts of James IV, James V and James VI, had reached a new and wider audience. In the process, it had undergone a change of character; the foundation was laid for a renaissance of letters. Its location was not the court but the libraries of the middling sort. It was a reflection of the instinctive reaction of a society in a process of rapid and often bewildering change, to rediscover its links with the past. Never before – or perhaps since – had both the works of vernacular Scots and histories of Scotland been so popular.

This was the most novel and, in the longer term, the most important of the three tributaries of the Scottish Renaissance. The best-known, not surprisingly, is that which was attached to the royal court. Kings had long been patrons of historians: Boece and his translator Bellenden, both pensioners of James V, belonged to a line of royal clients which stretched back to John of Fordun and beyond. The royal court was the focus of the arts: the court of James IV was familiar with at least six languages, and the jealousies of one client, the poet William Dunbar, for another better-paid, the Italian alchemist, Damian, were the excuse for the poem, 'The Fenyeit Freir of Tungland'. The threads of Stewart cultural patronage ran through the whole of the sixteenth century: they linked musicians like Robert Carver, a canon of the new Chapel Royal at Stirling in the time of James IV, David Riccio, an Italian musician at Mary's court, or the English musicians, the Hudsons, at the court of James VI. The most distinguished poets of the sixteenth century were invariably clients of the court: William Dunbar, Thomas Fowler, Alexander Scott and Alexander Montgomerie graced the courts of the four Stewart monarchs of the sixteenth century.

The milieu of the court was the accompaniment against which the growing status of the monarchy was rehearsed. Poets, artists and musicians were the commentators on the rise to new, European status of the Stewart dynasty. The venues were the palaces on which James IV and V spent formidable sums – Stirling Castle, with its 'palatium' or great hall, a royal chapel elevated into new status as a Chapel Royal in the reign of James IV, and a Renaissance-style palace with formal apartments constructed by his son; Linlithgow, vastly extended by James V so that it looked, according to his second bride, Mary of Guise-Lorraine, like a château on the Loire. Here, the cult of honour was displayed. James IV staged the Tournament of the White Knight and the Black Lady at Holyrood in 1507. It was greeted with such acclaim throughout Europe that it was performed again in the following year. It was before the court of James V that Lindsay's *Satire of the Three Estates* was first performed, in the open air at the Greenside beside Edinburgh in 1539; it was restaged in the Great Hall at Linlithgow a year later. The baptism at Stirling of the son of Mary, Queen of Scots in December 1566 was the occasion for a full-scale Renaissance triumph, the first ever staged in Britain, which combined spectacle, the literature of four languages – Latin, French, Italian and Scots – and the arts of war to convey the message that only the Stewart dynasty could bring peace to a troubled land. And the baptism in 1594 of Henry, first son of James VI, staged again at Stirling, was, with a tax of £100,000 Scots levied to pay for it, the single most expensive event in sixteenth-century Scotland. The costs of the cultivation of monarchy were rising massively, but so were monarchs' expectations of the loyalty due them by their subjects.

The astonishing range of the achievements of the Stewart court are testimony to two important points. In the sixteenth century, Scotland had a monarchy which was self-confident, ebullient and aggressive. In the politics of the British Isles, this was Scotland's century; from the moment the first son of Henry VII died in 1502, a

Stewart was only one or two heartbeats away from succession to the English throne. Henry VII's heir had been called Arthur; it was no accident that both James IV and V had sons whom they named Arthur or that James VI, when he succeeded to the English thone in 1603, considered changing his name to Arthur. English ambassadors were forced, grim-faced, to sit 'at a round table like Arthur's' by James IV; another round table was in 1566 a centre-piece of the celebrations of the birth of a young prince whose birthright, so the muses recited, would be to 'extend the territory of your realm, until the Britons will learn to unite in one kingdom'. The royal Renaissance of the sixteenth century was a weapon of diplomacy as well as a reflection of the glory of the monarchy. It also ensured that for much of that century the focus of Scottish culture lay firmly within the court.

The nobility were also able to bask in the reflected sunlight of the royal court. The cult of honour assured them of their place in the community of the realm, amidst and despite the myriad of social and economic change which the century brought with it. Much of the royal building programme had taken place in the half century between 1490 and 1540. The half century after 1590 was the period of a wider Scottish architectural renaissance, organised by nobles old and new. It saw the building by the Earl of Bothwell of an elaborate Italian façade within the structure of a fourteenth-century castle at Crichton; Fyvie Castle in Aberdeenshire was one of the most delightful of many examples of the change from tower house built for defence to a château built for gracious living, often surrounded by formal gardens; the Argyll Lodging in Stirling, a three-storey French-style hôtel around a courtyard, designed for Sir William Alexander, earl of Stirling, was a country house built within a town. Each was a symbol of a new leisured, landed class.

The nobility were as anxious to secure their roots in the past as their status in the present. This was the period when many histories of noble houses were written and genealogies, both real and counterfeit, were commissioned. The blind poet and lawyer, Sir Richard Maitland, wrote histories of the families of Seton and Wedderburn; the radical presbyterian laird, David Hume of Godscroft, wrote for his patron the Earl of Angus a history of the houses of Douglas and Angus, which was eventually published in 1644. The ambitious Campbell laird of Glenorchy had a collection of twenty-four pictures of kings and queens of Scotland, but he also had thirty-four portraits of 'lairds and ladies' drawn from his ancestors as well as a 'grit genealogie bord', painted by the royal artist George Jamesone. In sum, Scotland had not one Renaissance of the sixteenth century but three. Monarchs, nobles and the many layers of the middling sort each had its own. The departure of the court for London after the succession of James VI to the English throne tilted the balance between the three strands. The void left after the removal of the royal court was not made good by a country-house culture; except in Gaeldom, the nobility, intent on the recasting of the cult of honour, offered little in the way of wider literary patronage. There was, as a result, less creative writing of quality, in Scots or English, in the seventeenth century than in the sixteenth. Yet the impact of the printing press was to make available the great literary works of past generations to a new, wider reading public and to cultivate a distinctive sense of patriotism, grounded in Scotland's past – its kings, its learning and its literature, both vernacular and Latin. Already before 1603, despite official attempts to keep control of it, the printing press had become an instrument of a mass culture of various kinds. It would in the course of the seventeenth century produce an intelligentsia, largely made up of the middling sort of society. The result was a renaissance of letters, with its focus not in vernacular literature but in the wider world of scholarship, music, architecture, heraldry and the like.

The Reformation had to take account of this multi-layered Renaissance. Protestantism was, it has often been said, the religion of the book, and the evangelisation of society could move only at the pace that literacy, learning or political patronage would allow. The Protestant reformers would alternately look to a godly prince, the lesser magistrates and an educated godly society to implement religious reform. In his *History of the Reformation*, John Knox had begun his story in 1432, with the martyrdom of Paul Craw, a Bohemian teacher at the new University of St Andrews. Within the space of 300 words, he had reached the Lollards of Kyle in the 1490s and within a further thousand words the death in 1527 of another teacher at St Andrews, the talented young Lutheran theologian, Patrick Hamilton, 'with whom our History doth begin'. Although it was written during the personal reign of a Catholic queen, there was none the less no room in Knox's work for the conventional flattery of great noble houses, even though he did see the magnates as the 'chief pillars' of the Reformation.

The Reformation was more and less than a simple, single cataclysmic event. Scotland had two Reformations, in 1560 and 1567, and two Reformation settlements. The first had resulted from the concerted protest of a loose coalition of the 'Lords of the Congregation professing Christ Jesus' against French influence in government, but its leaders took pains to stress that they were not rebels against their Queen. It had taken its course without a detailed programme of Protestant reform. That, the *First Book of Discipline*, was drawn up only after the revolt was over. The eventual blueprint for a Protestant Reformation, an impressive but untidy document which had taken over eight months and at least two committees comprising a total of six ministers to devise, was too late to be presented to the Reformation Parliament of August 1560 and was never formally ratified, either by the Queen or by Parliament. The result was that the new Protestant Church found itself in something of a limbo. Its progress after 1560 was dramatic in some aspects, mixed in others. Its most impressive early achievement was the setting up of a reformed ministry and the erection of a disciplinary court, the kirk session; it and the parish remained the chief organ of Scotland's local government until the nineteenth century. By the end of 1561, 240 of Scotland's 1,080 parishes had been filled, and by 1567 they were served by about 850 clergy. Still, however, three-quarters of the ministry were made up of readers and exhorters rather than ministers proper, and neither kirk sessions nor (with the single exception of John Carswell's 1567 translation of the Genevan Book of Common Order) Protestant works in Gaelic would reach the Highlands until the seventeenth century.

The work justifying the revolution of 1567, the *History* of George Buchanan, moderator of the General Assembly at the time, was a very different apologia from that of Knox's. It found justification in the long line of kings supposedly censured by their nobles. There was a 'party of revolution' in 1567, which was more cohesive and determined than the coalition of 1559–60. It had the desperation born of an act of clear rebellion – the deposing of a queen and the coronation of a pretender, in the shape of the thirteen-month-old godly prince, who had been baptised Charles James in 1566 but was crowned James VI.

The General Assembly in 1567, meeting in the heady atmosphere only ten days after Mary's defeat at Carberry, set about the task of a second Reformation: it had to 'rebuild the ruinous house of God', root out 'superstition and idolatry' and secure a 'perpetual order' for the Church. The 'foundation stone', it claimed, had been laid in 1560 but the 'kaipstane' (coping stone) had still to be added. The result was more avowedly Calvinist than the Reformation of 1560, which had had as its centrepiece a Confession of Faith, which was the work of Knox but skilfully compiled to embrace the many different ideological influences – Lutheran and Zwinglian as well as Calvinist – which had played on Scottish Protestantism up to that date. There was, however, no new manifesto – even though parts of the *First Book of Discipline* were recognised to be out of date and the *Second Book* lay ten years into the future. The road which it took was a reaction against the experiences of the years of Mary, when the chief patron of a Protestant Church had been a Catholic queen. The Kirk had already had its first lesson in the dangers of Erastianism.

The year 1567 was a revolution in ways in which the Reformation of 1560, with its half-hidden compromises, was not. It looked to the nobles for support and especially to another royal Stewart, Mary's illegitimate half-brother the Earl of Moray, to act as a 'captain of Israel' to lead it into the promised land. The experience of the civil war which followed between 1568 and 1573, fought largely between rival noble coalitions labelled 'king's men' and 'queen's men', cautioned the Church about the wisdom of putting its faith in nobles. And the experience of Morton's regency (1572–8) after the war led Protestant Church to distance itself from Protestant State.

The *annus mirabilis* of 1567, which had established a short-lived alliance between godly Church and State, lived on – as the ideal which Calvinist dissidents in 1582, 1584, 1596 and 1638 looked back to. The Church, in search of a continuing Reformation, rejected the creature of its own making – the godly prince James VI. In his place, and despite its earlier disappointments, the reformed Church had by the 1630s again turned to the nobles as the 'little nursing fathers', as Samuel Rutherford called them, to push through what it saw as a new Reformation. The backbone of the revolt against Charles I was, however, the lawyers, lairds and ministers of the middling sort. A whole day, it is true, was set aside for the nobles to make their way to Greyfriars Church in Edinburgh to subscribe the Covenant; it was only on the second day that the rest of society was allowed in to sign it. But the Covenant was also the symbol of where intellectual leadership lay in post-union Scotland; it had been drawn up by Alexander Henderson, an Edinburgh minister, and Archibald Johnston of Wariston, a lawyer who was also a laird and originated from an Edinburgh merchant family.

In 1633, Charles I had passed under another elaborate structure, the 'Arch of Genealogy", which depicted his 107 predecessors. It was symbolic of the fact that kingship had long been the guarantor of Scottish independence. Since 1603, however, the most conservative institution in Scottish society had become the most radical: in place of a Scottish kingdom the Stewart monarchy had postulated a British state. By the 1630s, the reformed Church had emerged as a new, alternative symbol of Scottish nationhood. The Reformation of 1560, despite its calculated appeal to patriotism, had been a revolt of the provinces which had found it difficult to recast itself as a national rebellion. The campaign against the Prayer Book in 1637–8 would, by contrast, be an avowedly national movement. In the early 1560s, the General Assembly had often seemed to be only the forum for different 'cuntries' or localities: by 1638, it was a surrogate parliament. The reformers' abolition of saints in 1560 had threatened to cut the new Church of Scotland off from Scotland's past. By the 1620s and 1630s, histories of Scotland, like that written by the minister David Calderwood, had replaced the historical myth of the line of kings stretching back into pre-history with another – that of a link between the primitive, New Testament Church of the presbyterians with the early Celtic Church. Charles I, cultivating a more stylized Renaissance kingship, offered himself as a godly prince still, but of a Church which embraced all three of his kingdoms. The Kirk, exploiting the new wave of patriotic literature of a different and wider Scottish Renaissance, offered itself as the conservator of Scotland's constitution. Renaissance and Reformation had intertwined once again, but with startling new results. Many of them are with us still.

Twilight before night or darkness before dawn?
Interpreting seventeenth-century Scotland

DAVID STEVENSON

Honorary Research Professor, St Andrews University

THE SEVENTEENTH CENTURY in Scotland has had few friends. Traditionally, since the eighteenth century, it has been interpreted as a peculiarly unhappy age in Scotland's turbulent story, marked by cultural failure, religious fanaticism, economic decay, political violence and corruption, lacking any clear positive identity to offset these negative characteristics. This is all the more marked as the century is sandwiched between two which have strong identities. The sixteenth is dominated by Reformation and Renaissance, the eighteenth by Improvement and Enlightenment. The seventeenth often seems the awkward bit in between, with no similar dominant theme to give it unity. In popular history, the sixteenth and eighteenth centuries are illuminated respectively by the dazzling flares of Mary Queen of Scots and Bonnie Prince Charlie and their lost causes. The seventeenth century offers linking symbols of romantic failure in the persons of the Marquis of Montrose and Viscount Dundee, but they are pale and shadowy by contrast, casting only fitful light.

Yet though Scotland's seventeenth-century experience is frequently seen as repellent, this does not mean there is agreement about its significance – or lack of it – as a sort of grotesque interlude between the great ages of Reformation and Enlightenment. Historians of the two diametrically opposed main-line traditions in interpreting Scotland's past have, indeed, found common ground in rubbishing the seventeenth century – though for very different reasons.

Historians use centuries as convenient shorthand terms for distinctive periods in the past, often taking considerable liberties with precise dates in the process. But Scotland's historical seventeenth century conforms fairly closely to the chronological one: it runs from the Union of the Crowns in 1603 to the Union of the Parliaments in 1707. Differing attitudes to the latter event often influence or even determine attitudes to the whole century. To those in the nationalist tradition the age preceding 1707 in Scotland is discredited by that great betrayal, by the willingness of a majority of members of the country's political and social élites (as represented in the last Scottish Parliament) to vote away her sovereignty. In this perspective the seventeenth century becomes the age in which the traditional rulers of the country were corrupted by close links with England under the Union of the Crowns. It was the twilight of Scottish independence, in which her élites came to take English dominance for granted, and which culminated in their dereliction of duty in surrendering the country's hard-won independence. They failed the Scottish people by refusing to take account of the latter's patriotic hostility to the new incorporating Union. Thus the century of the Union of the Crowns was Scotland's dim twilight age before the long black night of Union fell, a grim age in which the forces of élite perfidy prepared themselves for the final treachery.

Historians in the rival unionist tradition have agreed on the blackness of the age. For them, the seventeenth century in Scotland was one of increasing poverty, oppression and violence, a century in which, if anything, these traditional badges of the country's backwardness and barbarism were even more marked than in previous centuries. But salvation was at hand, for the gloom of this age was the intensified darkness which precedes the dawn. The dawn was, of course, the incorporating Union with England, bringing archaic Scotland into a modern world of progress so that she could blossom into a new era of better and more stable government, economic improvement and Enlightenment. And looking further ahead, as the low morning sun rose higher in the sky, Scotland was – through 1707 and the rejection of her discredited past – freed to play a full part in the glories of the British world-empire on which the sun never set. She had achieved her destiny, not as a struggling independent state doomed to insignificance, but through acceptance of a British and imperial rôle.

As the Union of 1707 has lasted (up to the present at least), the unionist distortion of Scotland's seventeenth century has generally prevailed over the nationalist one, and its tentacles have spread to all aspects of Scotland's past in ways designed (though usually unconsciously) to reconcile Scots to the decision made in 1707. In considering subsequent positive or 'progressive' developments in the Scottish experience, there has been a strong tendency to take 1707 as a starting point, the unexamined assumption being that everything creditable in eighteenth-century Scotland flowed from the Treaty of Union, directly or indirectly. Agricultural improvement, the eventual flourishing of trade and industry, political stability, parliamentary government, the rule of law, Enlightenment: all have more often been seen in terms of breaks with Scotland's past than as developments evolving from that past. Study of pre-1707 Scotland, in this perspective, is little more than antiquarian indulgence, for the burden of her past was excess baggage sensibly jettisoned so that Scotland, as part of a new Britain, could embrace England's historical experience as more relevant to the future. Above all else perhaps, English constitutional history was transformed into British constitutional history. In theory in 1707 both Scottish and English Parliaments were abolished, a new institution, the British Parliament, created. In reality, of course, the English Parliament continued to exist, its traditions, powers and procedures unchanged except that a few new members representing Scotland were added to it. Scotland contributed nothing to the new state's constitution: her native parliamentary tradition was a discredited irrelevance. Surely, therefore, it was obvious that when Scots were taught constitutional history it should be the 'English' constitution they lived under that was explained to them.

Scotland's seventeenth century: dark, repellent, irrelevant, worth nothing more than a hasty glance to demonstrate how awful life had been before the Scots wisely embraced Union? Or a sad age of creeping betrayal of national destiny? Does Scottish History, 1603-1707, really matter no more than this?

The answer is a resounding denial of this suggestion, and this must be whether the personal perspective is unionist, nationalist or couldn't care less. At last in recent decades the seventeenth-century experience has begun to be re-assessed, and the century turns out to be vastly more diverse, exciting and interesting than it had previously seemed. It remains in many respects a profoundly unhappy century for Scotland, but her attempts to cope with the problems she faced emerge as fascinating, and it is now clear that 1707 does not mark the point at which the Scots wrote off their past and began new history within Britain, based on adoption of England's historical legacy. Culturally, it is true, the century was far from distinguished; anglicisation largely destroyed much of the native literary tradition, and the dominance of narrow and gloomy religious literature tends to repel. Yet historians of the Enlightenment now reach far back into the century in seeking to trace its origins, and find plenty of evidence of modest cultural and intellectual achievement as fanaticism gradually declines and men's interests broaden out into new secular fields.

In the economy there is considerable development in trade and industry in the course of the century. This is sporadic, and serious trading problems appeared in the last decade of the century, making a major contribution towards forcing the Scots to accept Union with England in 1707; but nonetheless, the slow, piecemeal changes which were taking place were preparing the way for the massive expansion that was to begin in the mid-eighteenth century. In agriculture the picture is similar. Many of the types of reform which were eventually to transform the Scottish countryside were already under discussion and even being put into practice in the seventeenth century. They were not implemented on a large scale, but nonetheless did contribute to a significant if unspectacular rise in agricultural productivity – though again this continuity has been disguised by short-term problems at the end of the century – a massively demoralising series of catastrophic harvest failures resulting from bad weather in the later 1690s, which caused the worst famine to hit the country for generations.

Changes in agriculture obviously reflected changing priorities in Scotland's dominant landed élites, moves away from the old 'lordship' society dominated by ties of kinship and feudalism in which manpower gave status, to a more commercial ethos in which money revenues came first. The involvement of many landlords in industrial and trading ventures confirms the trend. Along with commercialisation came anglicisation: under the Union of the Crowns Scots landlords had the choice of either retaining their distinct identity, but paying the price of being reduced to a provincial nobility, or assimilating to the English landed classes. Eventually, though often reluctantly, they chose assimilation, an anglicisation of attitudes and culture that they hoped would gain them status at court in London. Though little studied as yet, it is clear that this slow, unspectacular process of assimilation was central to the coming of political Union in 1707. It was (from the nationalist perspective) an insidious process that alienated them from the mass of the population of Scotland, and made their great betrayal of the country possible – or (switching to a unionist viewpoint), it was the rational acceptance of the superiority of things English that allowed the Scots élites to abandon narrow, outmoded national prejudices and set their country on a new course.

This brings us to what is perhaps the most central of the many themes of seventeenth-century Scottish history, and indeed perhaps of all Scottish history since the early kingdoms within the island of Britain had coalesced into two dominant political systems: the question of relations with England. Here, study of Scottish history is of significance not merely to Scots: it is vital to the understanding of England's political evolution in the course of the century, and of the development of the concept (and, eventually, the reality) of Britain.

Two kingdoms uneasily sharing one island, differing greatly in population and wealth. The generalisation applies that, whether considering individuals or nations, quarrels with neighbours are more likely than with anyone else, because neighbours have most contacts with each other and thus most possible occasions for conflict. If they had been left to fight it out between themselves, it is quite possible that a solution would have been found in English conquest and absorption of Scotland. Scotland escaped through the obvious strategy of a lesser power threatened by a great neighbour: ally with another neighbour at odds with your enemy – in this case, France. Thus Scotland preserved a precarious independence. By the sixteenth century, however, some Scots were wondering if the price was too high. Alliance with France was intended to protect them from English aggression, but if the French were to aid the Scots, the Scots in turn had to aid them: Scotland found herself involved in disastrous military enterprises – culminating in shattering defeats at Flodden (1513) and Solway Moss (1542) – more as a pawn in French wars with England than through protecting her own independence. Unease at increasing French domination of Scottish affairs peaked in the 1550s when the country was ruled by a French regent and her Crown seemed destined to be united with that of France. Fear of becoming a French province was central to the 1559-60 Reformation/Revolution which brought to power a Protestant, pro-English régime. But escape from a French frying-pan was possible only through risking immolation in an English fire. The overthrow of the French was made possible through English military intervention. In 1573 the English intervened again, to support a tottering Protestant regency, and on other occasions during the minority of the young James VI English influence was exerted against threatened Counter-Reformation. Even when James achieved adulthood he was both financially and politically dependant on the good will of Elizabeth of England, and though he strove to be his own man there is, in late sixteenth-century Scotland, more than a whiff of clientship – of Scotland, in spite of her formal independence, becoming informally a client or satellite state. This was made bearable to James and his subjects by two considerations: first, through recognition that friendship with England was central to the survival of a Protestant régime, the two countries having a common interest in resisting Catholic threats: second, and more positively, by the likelihood that James would succeed Elizabeth on the English throne. To have a Scot seated on the throne of England, the throne of Edward I and Henry VIII whose attempts to conquer Scotland had ended in failure, would be an ironic historical achievement for which it was well worth putting up with temporary humiliations.

This great hope achieved fruition in 1603. Edward I might have hijacked the symbol of the Scottish monarchy, the Stone of Scone, but now a Scotsman sat on the English throne that enclosed it. But what was Scotland's future to be in the new dual monarchy? In constitutional terms there were, basically, three alternatives. The first option was that England and Scotland should remain separate in government, politics, religion, culture, etc. Accident of inheritance meant that the two kingdoms shared the same monarch, and this would insure peace and stability in their relations with each other. This was what most Scots wanted and expected: two equal partners under one monarch.

The second choice was that the kingdoms should remain distinct, but the dominance of England – based on wealth and population as well as on historical claims to the overlordship of Scotland – would be recognised. Scotland's relationship with England would come to have many similarities to that of Ireland – separate but subordinate and dependent kingdom to be anglicised and to be ruled in England's interests. Not surprisingly this was an option that appealed to the English, but not to the Scots.

The third choice was that the two kingdoms could be completely merged to form a new, single state.

These issues were commonplace in European history. Most existing states of any size had grown out of the amalgamations of small-er political units in the past, brought together by conquest or the results (accidental or intended) of dynastic marriages in earlier gen-erations. And these provided many precedents and parallels relevant to what Britain was now beginning to experience. Most of them should have led thoughtful Scots to fear for their country's future. Certainly it had been common for centuries for rulers of composite states and multiple monarchies to accept diversity, that formerly independent units could retain their own institutions, laws, lan-guages, customs. Nonetheless, smaller units which became attached to larger ones almost invariably found themselves ruled in the inter-ests of the greater. Moreover, by this time emerging absolutist theo-ries of political authority were tending to stress the advantages of uniformity in territories under a single ruler – and obviously the model for such uniformity tended to be the greater unit which formed the core of the monarchy. Imposing greater uniformity was intended to make provincial revolts less likely – but in the short term it often provoked them.

So dynastic ambition was realised in 1603: as far as James was concerned, the destiny of Scotland's ancient race of kings had at last been fulfilled in the divinely ordained Union of Britain under his rule. Yet surely some people saw the ominous relevance of one con-tinental precedent to Scotland's case. The Burgundian dynasty which ruled the Netherlands had inherited the crown of Spain. It was taken for granted that the dynasty would rule from what was now its greatest territory, Castile, at the heart of the Spanish monar-chy – just as nobody questioned that King James would rule Britain from London. An alien dynasty took over Spain, but within a gener-ation it had 'gone native', and was coming to be seen as alien by its Dutch subjects: it was regarded as ruling them in Spanish interests. The result was the great Revolt of the Netherlands, beginning in the 1560s: and in 1603 the Dutch were still fighting to gain indepen-dence from absentee rule from Spain.

The attitude of King James himself was that Union of the king-doms and people should logically, and indeed automatically, follow from the Union of the Crowns, and he devoted much wordy rhetoric (though it was distinctly vague about details) to trying to persuade his subjects of this. He failed. Mutual suspicions between the two peoples were too strong: Scotsmen feared absorption into England;

Englishmen feared being dominated by Scots favoured by their royal compatriot. Though James's attempts at 'complete' Union were thwarted, the fact that he made them suggests that he foresaw difficulties in trying to rule the kingdoms separately in ways which would keep both happy. Events were to prove him right – but the alternative policies he adopted when his Union plans failed contributed greatly to this outcome. Since he had to rule the kingdoms separately, he resolved to seek to make them as like each other as possible. Conflict between them would become less likely as they became more alike, and perhaps eventually they would be so similar that objections to political Union would collapse. In practice uniformity meant no change for England, but anglicisation for Scotland. This was most clearly seen, and most resented, in religion. The two kingdoms might be bound together by common Protestantism, but simultaneously they were held apart by the different ways in which their national churches had developed. Resentment in Scotland intensified when James's son, Charles I, accelerated his father's policies, greatly increasing the demands he made on his Scottish subjects for obedience to unpopular and frequently anglicising policies.

The result was the great national revolt which began in Scotland in 1637 – and which had many similarities with the revolts of Catalonia and Portugal against Castilian domination in 1640. Religion legitimised revolt, providing an ideology that united Scots at all levels of society against their native, but now alien, dynasty. Their defiance, aimed at the king and his advisers and not at the English, was remarkably successful: for once the English sympathised with the Scots and obstructed his attempts to fight them.

By 1641 the Scots had achieved religious and constitutional revolution, creating a presbyterian Church and a Parliament free from royal control. King Charles had to accept being reduced to a figurehead. But the Scots rebels, the Covenanters, now had an even more challenging role to perform, one that verged on the impossible. They accepted continuing political links with England – not least because these seemed unbreakable unless the dynasty was dethroned north of the border, and this was inconceivable; it might be anglicised, but it was Scots in origin, and central to the country's national identity. Therefore instead of rejecting the Union of the Crowns, the Scots set out to remodel it so that Scotland could play her rightful rôle within it. What was envisaged was a loose federal arrangement, with royal power strictly limited by Parliaments in each kingdom, and a joint body of an equal number of commissioners from each kingdom supervising matters of joint concern – such as relations between the kingdoms and foreign policy. From the Scottish perspective a fair Union with England involved equal partnership of this sort.

Inevitably, however, and understandably, from an English perspective such a partnership seemed most unfair. It would give the fewer than one million Scots the same power in joint affairs as the more than five million Englishmen and Welshmen: and the discrepancy in wealth between the two nations was much wider still. The Scots were, it seemed, trying to follow up victory over the king by seizing a totally disproportionate power in British affairs. Other aspects of Scottish ambitions emphasised this further. In religion, they demanded the Scotticisation of England and Ireland – the imposition of presbyterianism. Just as much as James VI and Charles I, they took it for granted that politics and religion were inseparable, and that stable friendship in the former sphere necessitated uniformity in the latter. Yet at first the prospect for what amounted, in English eyes, to Scottish domination of Britain, seemed good. After defeating the king in England the Covenanters forced him to summon parliament in England, to give his English enemies a forum in which to attack his power. Thus the famous Long Parliament, which was to push through an English constitutional revolution and then defeat the king in a bloody civil war, was summoned at the behest of the Scots: and a number of the most important constitutional reforms it introduced were based on recent Scottish legislation. English parliamentarians admitted that they owed their liberties to the Scots, and their dependence on the Scots was such that they were willing to make promises – if rather vague ones – to reform religion and the Union on Scots lines.

The Scots fancied themselves as controllers of events, ring-masters of Britain's three-kingdom three-ring circus, but the performers were soon spinning wildly, beyond anyone's control. First Ireland and then England, destabilised by the destruction of royal power by the Scots, collapsed into civil war. At the request of the English parliament the Covenanters sent armies into both kingdoms. Though this was an immense drain on Scotland's resources, the Covenanters reconciled themselves to it with the argument that it increased the

English Parliament's dependence on the help of the Scots, and thus would strengthen their ability to impose the Scots variant of equal Union on Britain.

They were deluding themselves. Predictably, once the Scots had helped the English Parliament win the civil war, that Parliament forgot the promises the Scots had exacted from it as the price of military aid. Bitterly disillusioned, the Scots sought repeatedly and increasingly desperately to force the English into a Scots-dominated settlement. The result was, eventually, to exasperate the English under Oliver Cromwell into invading and conquering Scotland (1650-1) and imposing what they understood to be equal Union: a political Union with a single British Parliament in which only a small proportion of the members were Scots. As England had many times the population and wealth of Scotland, this had to be reflected in the membership of a joint legislature if power was to be justly distributed between the two nations.

By revolting against anglicisation the Scots thus ended up with amalgamation with England, and far more thorough anglicisation under Cromwell's republican régime than they had ever suffered under Charles I. Monarchy was soon restored, it is true, in the person of Charles II in 1660, and the hated 'incorporating' Union disappeared as Union of the Crowns returned. But the great mid-century upheaval had deeply seared the Scots' psyche. In 1637 they had had the confidence to take their destiny in their own hands, and to seek to re-model Britain to their liking. The result had been years of bloodshed and destruction culminating in the utter disaster of conquest. The national myth that Scotland was the never-conquered nation had frequently given Scots heart in hard times in the past: now it had been shattered for ever. So too, for the great majority, had the awe-inspiring belief, which had reached its apogee under the Covenanters, that the Scots were the successors to the Jews as a chosen people of God, to whom he would bring victory, whatever the odds, in doing His work on earth. Harsh reality had proved that in Britain the tail could not wag the dog – or at least only very briefly, when the English dog had been thrown off balance by internal illness. Their lesson was learnt well. Scotland followed England's lead both in restoring monarchy in 1660 and in overthrowing a tyrannical and incompetent ruler – James VII – in 1688, rather than risk taking the initiative herself. And though the Scots did try again to assert their vision of their rightful place within the Union of the Crowns after 1688, when this led to a situation in which open conflict with England was likely, they gave way to an essentially English-dictated, incorporating Union (sweetened with concessions on free trade, law and religion).

Seen in one context, Scotland's experience in the seventeenth century is a classic example of the problems of a small state within a multiple monarchy. In another, understanding of it is essential to understanding the emergence of the kingom of Great Britain. A nation *is* its past, and to comprehend what it means to be British it is necessary to take seriously the pasts of Scotland, Ireland and Wales as well as of England – as British historians, encouragingly, are increasingly accepting. Perhaps one day 'British' history, meaning 'English history, with some mention of the tiresome Scots, Irish and Welsh when they are making a nuisance of themselves' will finally be buried. Finally, just as it is entirely legitimate for the English and others to study English history in its own right – provided it is not called British – so equally it is important to study Scottish history to understand what it means to be Scots, and how to place the country in wider British and European historical contexts.

For some, whose political hearts rule their historical perceptions, the seventeenth century in Scotland will remain stereotyped: darkness before dawn or twilight before night. They are missing a lot. This complex century has many inter-twined themes, most of which cannot find space for even a mention in this short essay. The real darkness comes not from the nature of developments in the century, but from lack of modern historical research. To put this positively, the opportunities for research are many and exciting, and the probing torch-beams of specialist studies are beginning to criss-cross and merge into wider illumination of broad areas.

Union, Jacobitism and Enlightenment

BRUCE P. LENMAN
Professor of Modern History, St Andrews University

THE INCORPORATING UNION of 1707 casts a long shadow in Scottish history, both backwards and forwards. Most people can recognise its centrality in the endless, and, in the last decade of the twentieth century, increasingly intense debate within Scottish society on Scottish identity, but fewer realise that all Scottish politics after 1688 were shadowed by the prospect of some form of Union. The Revolution of 1688 in Scotland was quite different from the Glorious Revolution in England, as indeed was the Revolution in Ireland or that in the provinces of the English nation in America. Only the events in Old England could be described as glorious because bloodless. In Scotland, the struggle for some sort of settlement after the ousting of James VII dragged on from 1688 to 1690 and included a blessedly brief, but bloody civil war in the shape of the first Jacobite rising, launched against the authority of the Estates (or Parliament) of Scotland by John Graham of Claverhouse,Viscount Dundee.

The drama of that rising, and in particular of Dundee's death in the moment of victory at Killiecrankie, has tended to obscure facts and developments which were in the long run much more significant. William of Orange was uninterested in Scotland. It is no accident that his first communication to the Estates of Scotland urged them to devote their attention to a Union with England. The reply of the Estates was as shrewd as it was dignified: there were more urgent tasks such as securing the religion and liberties of the realm from any repetition of the assaults to which they had been subjected by Stuart tyranny. William III was disappointed, for he had come to save Stuart government from the follies of James VII and II rather than the British peoples from that government. Even before the majestic cadences of Macaulay started to reverberate round the collective consciousness of the south-east-of-England-centred British establishment, William III was seen as one of the founders of England's greatness. Under his sceptre England became a parliamentary monarchy, a European great power, and a booming commercial country preparing itself for eventual industrial 'take-off'. The picture, even in England, is over-simple, but in Scotland the image of Dutch William was always very much less favourable.

He was rather a bad King of Scots, saved mainly by the fact that he was the only feasible Protestant candidate for the post of chief executive. Even his deeply loyal, and devoutly Protestant, General Hugh Mackay who, despite defeat at Killiecrankie, successfully destroyed the Jacobite challenge in a lengthy campaign, thought that the willingness of William to retain in office some of the most resented and soiled agents of King James was counter-productive and wrong. It soon became apparent to the Scots Estates that William was particularly attached to precisely those abuses, such as the use of a nominated committee of Lords of the Articles to emasculate the legislature, which had been most resented under King James. William eventually was forced to make concessions in 1688-90 by a remarkable combination between Jacobites and the extreme Whigs organised in what was known as 'The Club'. All the great constitutional concessions of the Revolution in Scotland were made grudgingly by a monarch who would have preferred to browbeat a divided opposition and bribe greedy individual politicians until he secured unconditional control. Men like Robert Fergusson 'the Plotter', who had been passionate advocates of the Glorious Revolution in England in 1688, could be accused of treasonable trafficking with Jacobitism in Scotland by 1690. There was no real inconsistency in his record. He considered that 'Revolution Principles' had been betrayed by the new executive and he knew that only co-operation between ideologically-divided opposition groups would produce results.

The Scottish political class of the late seventeenth century had two substantial achievements to its credit. Above all, it contrived to prevent Graham of Claverhouse from plunging the country into the welter of profitless bloodshed and destruction which James Grahame, fifth earl and first marquis of Montrose, had, with the assistance of Alasdair MacColla and his Ulster MacDonalds, inflicted on Scotland in 1644-45. Secondly, in 1689-90, with the aid of some brilliant individuals, it prised meaningful concessions out of a bitterly resentful executive. The only reason William agreed to concessions was that he meant to take them all back, using his right of initiative to abolish Scottish political institutions by engineering a Union with the Westminster ones. On his deathbed, his message to the Scotland he never saw and for which he cared so little was the one with which his reign had started: the need for incorporating Union.

His reign was the essential background to the eventual legislation of 1707 and, indeed, has been used by the latest significant English historian of the Act of Union of 1707, P. W. J. Riley, as the principal justification for it. In his two volumes, *King William and the Scottish Politicians* (Edinburgh, John Donald, 1979) and *The Union of England and Scotland* (Manchester, Manchester University Press, 1978) he adopts the simple device of arguing that the Scots magnates who dominated the nation's pre-1707 politics were such an utterly unprincipled, factious and irresponsible crew that the abolition of the Scots Parliament was the kindest thing that could be done for the Scots. In his own words, it is a bilious view of the Scots leadership, indeed a modern Black Legend of the kind which William S. Maltby studied in his *The Black Legend in England: the development of anti-Spanish sentiment, 1558-1660* (Duke University Press, Durham NC, 1971). That legend was created by early-modern English writers to justify assaults on Imperial Spain. Riley's legend is essentially a justification for the elimination of the Scottish political dimension in 1707. Such a legend involves far too much sleight of hand. In Riley's version of immediately pre-1707 Scottish politics, religion has to be a mere mask for self-interest. Often it was. Often it was not. All emphasis on the rôle of the executive in conjuring up political storms has to be eliminated. The massacre of Glencoe in 1692 was a vile business, but the central issue, as Andrew Fletcher of Saltoun said at the time, was that it showed that the government of King William made the same cynical and arbitrary use of force in the Highlands for political reasons as the government of King James. The report of the enquiry launched by the Scots Parliament into the massacre is a model of sane, civilised, honest discourse. The government's shielding and whitewashing of the principal offenders was in an already well-established stonewalling tradition.

In fact, few Englishmen have ever been interested in the Union of 1707. Dr Johnson said in 1769 that he was shocked to find that a certain man of eminence (described as a 'wit about town who wrote Latin bawdy verses') had no idea of the existence of the Act of Union

of 1707, and when A.V. Dicey and R. S. Tait published on the subject in 1920, they started their book with a section entitled 'First
Consideration – The ignorance, even of educated Englishmen, with
regard to the Act of Union of 1707'. In so far as it ever impinged on
the English mind, it tended to do so in the style of G. M. Trevelyan
or Sir Winston Churchill, both of whom took it for granted that it
was one of the glories of the reign of Good Queen Anne, helping to
secure the base from which England soared to become truly the
greatest of the Great Powers.

In theory, a new state called Great Britain, with a new legislature,
was created in 1707. In practice, Westminster swallowed a few
venal Scots MPs and even fewer venal Scots peers, and carried on as
before. Trevelyan wrote the history of *England under Queen Anne,*
and historians have continued to write histories of England cover-
ing periods long after the unions with Scotland or Ireland.
Churchill, with his Anglo-American vision (and delusions) wrote on
The History of the English-Speaking Peoples, but by that he meant the
England of his father and the America of his mother, with some ref-
erence to white settlement colonies which became Dominions. His
spell as Liberal MP for Dundee left little mark, apart from an enduring hatred of the local press baron, and it was appropriate that his
idea of a great Scotsman was the kenspeckle comedian, Harry
Lauder.

Apart from a spurt of interest amongst specialists like Dicey when
the Anglo-Irish Union was foundering, the Act of Union of 1707 has
remained a great bore among English scholars. That it was a pre-
arranged package rather than a genuine negotiation we have known
since the writings of the contemporary Jacobite George Lockhart of
Carnwath, and it was nice to have a conclusive demonstration from
Paul Scott, much more recently, that it was pushed over a crucial
hurdle as everyone had always suspected, by bribing the unworthy
Duke of Hamilton. However, that is not really why a reassessment
of the Act of Union of 1707 is desirable. Rather, it is necessary to
break the absurd assumption that the only conceivable future for
past generations was the one frozen in our present.

J. Steven Watson, who spent many years as principal of St
Andrews University, had a great deal more to say about Scottish par-
liamentarians in his study of *The Reign of George III* than about
Scotland, but then he built his career on the historical worship of

the Westminster Parliament. To him, any criticism levelled at Westminster was the Sin against the Holy Ghost. It was, before his death, a quaintly old-fashioned viewpoint derived from the days when a Britain Pre-Eminent was the Workshop of the World, and Westminster the unsurpassable peak of human political achievement. In the 1990s, a diminished United Kingdom steadily falling behind other industrial nations in relative economic performance, and with a form of government which most Americans and Western Europeans find bizarre if and when they bother to examine it in detail, needs a more appropriate and critical historiography. Political connections between Scotland, England, and be it said Ireland, are as inevitable as they are desirable, but their form and function are as susceptible to constructive analysis as any other man-made artefact, and a historiography deliberately designed to paralyse thought needs to be chased from the field.

The alternative to paralysing thought in a given field is, of course, to trivialise it. That, for many decades, was the fate of the literature surrounding the phenomenon of Jacobitism, to the point where one can sympathise with that irascible hereditary Whig Keeper of the Records of Scotland, Sir James Fergusson of Kilkerran, who once argued in print that the production of further narratives about the '45 should be a statutory offence carrying heavy penalties. He had a point, even if he also had his tongue in his cheek. In another work, Sir James argued that to the vast majority of Lowland Scots at the time the true tragedy of the '45 was that it ever happened. Certainly, the triumphant Whig intellectuals of the late Scottish Englightenment, like David Hume, wasted no tears on the defeated Jacobites. George I and George II naturally hated them. Yet with the accession of George III in 1760, the attitude of the British establishment changed significantly. The old, excluded and harassed Tory party of the reign of Queen Anne, or what was left of it, ceased to be a band of political untouchables. There had always been a Jacobite minority within it, but by 1760, Jacobitism was politically dead. The Young Pretender's brother, Prince Henry, had thrown in his hand by taking a cardinal's hat as early as 1747. Even the French dropped the exiled Stuarts after the naval battle of Quiberon Bay destroyed the last invasion scheme for which they had tentatively pencilled in Prince Charles as the figurehead.

Ex-Jacobites, old Tories, neo-Jacobites, were welcomed aboard the ship of state. The risings themselves were fading rapidly in the Establishment's consciousness. The '15 loomed through the mist of forgetfulness as a little local difficulty in the North of England, with the usual incomprehensible scuffle in Scotland. If anyone did remember the '19, it was as a comic-opera performance in a place remote even by Scottish standards. The '45 was an embarrassing freak by what everyone called 'the Highland Army', despite the fact that there were quite a few non-Highlanders in it. Even at the time of the '45, George II and the Duke of Cumberland regarded the rebellion as an irritating interruption to the serious business of continental European war. By the 1760s and 1770s, the ex-Jacobite Highland aristocracy were falling over themselves to organise their clansmen as cannon-fodder for the European and American wars of George III. An ex-Jacobite like Lord Mansfield could rise to be Lord Chief Justice of England whilst necessarily lying through his teeth about the Jacobite indiscretions of his youth. George III quite actively set out to incorporate into his image the high-flying authoritarian traditions of sacred kingship cultivated at the court of the exiled Stuarts. He even bought the exiled dynasty's relics and archives from the Cardinal Duke of York, who died his pensioner.

Incorporating grass-roots Jacobite support into the historical pedigree of the modern British establishment was much more difficult. One solution was to forget it, as did J. H. Plumb who wrote about the growth of political stability in a period when the British state faced a dangerous abortive Franco-Jacobite invasion in 1708; a massive rising in Scotland, with a subordinate English rising in 1715; rioting against the malt tax which required suppression by horse, foot and guns in Glasgow in the 1720s; the Porteous Riot in the Edinburgh of the 1730s; and panic in London with a rebel army at Derby late in 1745. So far from being stable, Hanoverian Britain teetered on the brink of potentially lethal violence at least once every decade in the first half of the eighteenth century.

And, on the whole, it did so because it deserved to. The virtual Whig putsch after the accession of George I left the natural majority party in the English nation, the Tories, deeply disgruntled. Robert Walpole was brought into office to stonewall attempts to probe the full scale of the involvement of the royal family and the government in the infamous South Sea Bubble. Under his régime, the first unmistakable emergence of the *over-mighty prime minister* occurred in British politics. In Scotland, where the '15 was regarded as the last of the wars of independence, hope for a drastic re-negotiation of the terms of association laid down in the Act of Union faded. Instead, the Walpole era spawned the rise of a crushing ascendancy over local politics and public patronage in the hands of the Argathelians, the followers of the Duke of Argyll. Resented by Westminster governments (which would have preferred to monop- olise and distribute patronage themselves), that ascendancy was challenged by the rival Whig faction called the Squadrone, but was cemented into place until 1761 by the tact and cunning of Archibald Campbell, Earl of Ilay and eventually third Duke of Argyll. The nar- rowness of the channels which allowed access to influence and favour in Scotland certainly drove some desperate men into sup- porting the '45. The groundswell of popular support for that unex- pected rising may have been confined largely to the Highlands and the North-East, but the profound apathy towards Westminster which enabled a handful of men to seize control in Scotland was vir- tually universal, and the march to Derby showed there was a lot of it around in England.

   In short, active Jacobitism was a popular critique, and a quite con- scious one, of British government. That was not how its ardent admirers in the nineteenth and early-twentieth centuries wanted to remember it. The tone was set by Walter Scott, whose Jacobite nov- els were designed not only to meet the needs of his own Hanoverian unionist politics, but also to reassert the nation's past as a means of preserving its identity – as well as to make money. They are designed to reconcile national animosities (which is why the 'history' in, say, Waverley, is so garbled and improbable even by the standards of later historical novelists). His second objective was more general: to pro- duce an antidote to the subversive radicalism which he feared might be the predominant political product of an urbanised, industrial society. Jacobites embodied loyalty, misguided loyalty no doubt, but wholly admirable loyalty because it was unquestioning loyalty to God-given social and political superiors. A wave of conservative antiquarian enthusiasm, rooted in this particular view, went on into the twentieth century, With great researchers like Alistair and Henrietta Tayler, the scholarship became so formidable and critical that the resulting books rise beyond any partisan loyalties to perma- nent value, but in someone like Sir Charles Petrie, writing in 1932, the original thrust of the school is apparent, as in the conclusion to the first edition of his book on *The Jacobite Movement,* where he said:

'. . . the spiritual heirs of the Jacobites in these islands are to be found among the followers of Mr Baldwin and among those of Mr De Valera . . .'

By this Petrie, an extreme right-wing English Roman Catholic, wished to imply that Jacobites would have backed the two very conservative Prime Ministers who between them dominated the British Isles in the 1930s, the Anglican Stanley Baldwin who ruled the United Kingdom of Great Britain and Northern Ireland, and the Roman Catholic Eamon de Valera who became Premier of the Irish Free State in 1932 and remained continuously in office until 1948. Both men were exponents of a backward-looking rhetoric idealizing a lost rural world. Both believed in minimal government.

Whether this sort of attempt to annex them for the cause of a standstill conservatism is fair to historic Jacobite activists is doubtful. A spiritual and political soporific Jacobitism was not. It was inspired by a fierce criticism of precisely the Westminster political system of which Scott was enamoured, and of which, incidentally, the government of the Republic of Ireland is a close copy. Its rulers always meant to retain a centralized parliamentary system in which a disciplined party majority could hand virtually unlimited internal power to a prime minister just as at Westminster. De Valera was very like the United Kingdom's premiers of the twentieth century whose authority has earned them the description of 'elected dictators'. Historic popular Jacobitism was passionately opposed to such centralized systems concentrating power in one minister. Hence Jacobite hostility to Sir Robert Walpole, the early eighteenth-century founder of the modern British premiership. Jacobites usually were socially conservative, but not politically deferential, as Prince Charles discovered, to his fury, in 1745-6. We need to face both the conservative and the radical strands in their thought if they are to be allowed a worthwhile place in our heritage.

Recent research has done much to clear the mists of ignorance which for long made specific Jacobite episodes either apparently grotesque, like the abortive Franco-Jacobite invasion of 1708, or difficult to explain, like the sudden launching of the '45 after a lengthy period of Jacobite passivity. In both these cases it has been by restoring the French dimension that it has been possible to see the logical structures underlying the course of events. The abortive '08 was designed to take advantage of the unpopularity of the Act of Union in Scotland to allow the Jacobite claimant, James Francis Edward Stuart, to seize control of that country, with the help of an internal rising and a French expeditionary force. He was then to help Louis XIV of France to escape from the crippling War of the Spanish Succession by rerunning the Bishops' Wars of 1639-40 against Charles I, by occupying the source of London's fuel supply in the Tyne-Tees coalfields, and thereby forcing the London government to the negotiating table. Incompetent navigation by the French admiral in command wrecked the scheme, not lack of a rational strategy.

Similarly, research on the origins of the '45 has moved from meticulous documentation of Scots Jacobite plotters of the 1730s (most of whom, for good reasons, did not come out in the '45) to an analysis of French policy in 1744. Prince Charles had been brought to the north coast of France to act as the Jacobite figurehead for a French invasion of southern England. The troops were to come from Flanders, and the commander was to be that fine soldier the Marshal de Saxe. It was the best and very probably the last chance of a Stuart restoration. The trouble was that the French went off the idea, not least because de Saxe himself was opposed to the withdrawal of French troops from a successful campaign in Flanders; to the idea of opening another front; and to the degree of risk involved in a seaborne invasion. In the summer of 1745 Prince Charles threw the dice by mounting a minuscule invasion of Scotland with only small-scale covert French backing, not because he originally thought the Scots could carry him triumphant to London, his objective, but because he hoped that the sight of a successful Scottish Jacobite rising would move Louis XV to reinstate the 1744 plan to invade England as a top priority.

Yet if the new Jacobite historiography has recreated the vital international context of the Jacobite risings (the '15 always excepted, because this greatest of the risings was always primarily domestic in nature), it has also shown tendencies to irrationality. Since the roots of this new school lay in the *History of Parliament* and the analysis of the correspondence of MPs, the temptation to construe any contact with the exiled Stuarts as a sign of committed Jacobitism, when often it was prudent fire insurance and no more, has proven irresistible. The rituals of English Jacobitism, that culture of alienation

from the Whig world which bred passive withdrawal rather than
rebellious action, have been well studied. Less satisfactory has been
a tendency to slide from records of correspondence, patterns of
memorials and toasts to implying that there was substantial, meaningful Jacobite support in England. This is programmatic history,
i.e. history as neo-Jacobite historians would have liked it to have
happened. English Jacobitism was largely a heritage of hot air. That
fact became apparent to the Scottish chiefs and generals during their
march into England in the winter of 1745, and was one of the major
motives behind their decision to turn back at Derby.

One scholar contends that the supreme heritage of Jacobitism was
the Scottish Enlightenment. His argument is a clever variation on
that advanced by the Victorian cultural historian, Thomas Henry
Buckle, whose detestation of Scottish Presbyterianism led him to
compare the backward and bigoted Scot and his Protestant traditions, with the urbanely rational Frenchman, whose civilisation has
a Roman Catholic background, and to conclude that the Frenchman
was better than his religion, while the Scot inherited a religious tradition too good for him. A similar bias can easily move on to argue
that Episcopalian Jacobites had to lie at the roots of the Scottish
Enlightenment, for only they were cosmopolitan enough (through
their experience of exile), and free enough from religious bigotry to
rise to levels of rationality acceptable in twentieth-century Oxford.
Though some ex-Jacobites, like the political economist Sir James
Steuart, were important figures in the era of the high Enlightenment,
the more general argument will not do.

The term 'Scottish Enlightenment' was apparently first invented
by William Robert Scott in 1900 and can therefore be seen as a modern label for an undoubted eighteenth-century phenomenon.
Different definitions of that phenomenon are possible, but no rep-
utable definition can duck the fact that in the 1760s, 1770s and
1780s, when the Enlightenment in Scotland was at the height of its
European reputation, it was, apart from a couple of atypical figures
like David Hume and Adam Smith, predominantly the achievement
of Presbyterian clergymen of the Moderate Party, or their close associates. It was far from being part of Peter Gay's Enlightenment, a
Europe-wide association of liberal, anti-establishment anti-clericals.
Even Gay's Enlightenment was far from socially subversive.
Voltaire, however much he criticized the Gallican Church or the

Parlement de Paris, never questioned the authority of the king or the privileges of the ruling élites. The Scottish Enlightenment was positively clerical and university-based, as well as politically and socially conservative. That description would apply particularly to the second half of the eighteenth century, and arises from a heavy emphasis on the *literati,* the men of letters, and those cultivated persons who associated with them and read them.

It is essential to broaden the chronological span of the Scottish Enlightenment. This does not violate its generally admitted central characteristics, such as a love of learning and virtue; a respect for faith and science; and a desire to elevate the social tone and international standing of Scotland by cultivating a refined cosmopolitan politeness of manner. All of that can be traced straight back to Restoration Scotland, when a restored aristocratic ascendancy sought after 1660 to create a conservative but lively intellectual culture comparable to that of other polite nations. Not for nothing was Sir William Bruce, a Royalist agent under Cromwell and a Jacobite under William III, hailed as 'the introducer of polite architecture into Scotland'. Lord Burlington's *protégé* Colin Campbell, who died in 1729, showed in his *Vitruvius Britannicus* that he believed that Bruce stood firmly in the apostolic succession of palladianism. The great Scots lawyers of the late seventeenth century, the institutionalists Viscount Stair and Mackenzie of Rosehaugh, shaped a tradition which ran continuously through the Revolution to the eighteenth century, and the very strong topographical and scientific interests of the Restoration, often pursued by physicians like Sir Robert Sibbald and Archibald Pitcairne, simply carried on into the later period, not least in the applied science practised mainly by eighteenth-century Scots physicians who had learned chemistry in the Netherlands at Leiden, where they sat at the feet of the great Boerhaave.

Of course, there were changes and developments. As the language used to gain access to an international audience, English replaced Latin. Episcopalianism was replaced by a Presbyterian church settlement. As a result, there were grave tensions, especially within the Scots aristocracy, but by the second half of the eighteenth century, the leaders of the Moderate clergy like Hugh Blair, John Home, William Robertson and Alexander Carlyle were working hard and successfully to adapt a Presbyterian establishment to the tone of a conservative society still dominated by its aristocracy. Finally, there

was a substantial change of literary emphasis with the rise of a
greater volume of publishing in fields such as moral philosophy and
political economy, not to mention *belles lettres*, and the emergence
of substantially new forms of writing such as philosophical history.

Of late, highly original work by David Allan in his *Virtue, Learning
and the Scottish Enlightenment* has returned historical writing in the
Scottish Enlightenment to a tradition much older than the late seventeenth and eighteenth centuries.   Allan has shown that the
Scottish historical tradition stretches with a high degree of continuity from Hector Boece, whose Latin *History of Scotland* was published in 1527, to well past 1800. Nor was the historical writing of
the period 1540–1750 fundamentally different from that of the
period 1750–1800 in the sense that all historians of substance
sought to establish themselves as moral legislators of the national
community, because they believed that history writing had an
improving social function. This was particularly true of the writers
who were members of the Moderate party in the Church of Scotland,
like Principal Robertson.

Of course, the precise objectives aimed at by Scots bent on national
improvement changed with time. Important reassessments of the
mental world of the Scots who supported the Act of Union of 1707
have underlined the extent to which that 'Union for Empire' was
designed to solve certain very specific problems, and to open up
discerned opportunities especially in the imperial field. It marked,
for example, an experiment for all who feared the violent heritage of
the wars of religion in the seventeenth-century British Isles, in the
creation of a multi-confessional polity balanced by a centralised
unitary state.   In many ways Scots Whigs were much more sin-
cerely attached to the idea of a new start and a new identity than
the English sponsors of the Union, for whom it was primarily a
device for ensuring security and abolishing Scottish politics at any
significant level.

Colin Kidd, in an important book on *Subverting Scotland's Past*,
has probed the whole question of the relationship between the
Scottish *literati* of the High Enlightenment and the manipulation of
post-Union Scottish identity. What emerges is the despair of many
leading figures in the Scottish Enlightenment when they contem-
plated their country's past. To them meaning in history was about
the growth of prosperity and civility. Since Scottish history seemed

to their ineffable condescension to be a record of barbarism and poverty, they placed themselves in the vanguard of the attempt to forge a new Anglo-British identity rooted in the Whig tradition. Interestingly, that enterprise never truly succeeded; the union state never created a monolithic British identity to match its political centralization. The term 'British' remained as ambiguous as ever, and totally compatible with other identities, some of them national. Union, as John Robertson has remarked, was an empirical option in 1707, and remains no more sacred than the Scottish sovereignty which it terminated. Yet the conservative *illuminati* of the period 1750-80, who were themselves passionately committed to that Union, did not see themselves as a given generation in a world of constant flux and change. However that might be true of individual fortunes, they saw their own ideas and the social context from which they sprang as part of a providential or inevitable progression which was irreversible and moved in an absolutely fixed direction.

Herein lies the most seductively dangerous dimension of the heritage of the Scottish Enlightenment. As Gladys Bryson pointed out in her classic study *Man and Society: the Scottish Inquiry of the Eighteenth Century,* first published in 1945, the writers of the high Enlightenment believed they could construct an empirical science of man, based on unchangeable 'facts of human nature', which facts they saw as an analogue to the chemist's elements. Their conclusions were general.They shunned the merely particular, reaching out for conclusions at once universal and eternal. Hence one can argue for Walter Scott, who died in 1832, and who was uniquely influenced by both the Enlightenment and Romanticism, as a truly terminal figure in the history of the Scottish Enlightenment, since Romanticism marked a huge shift in discourse towards the particular and the irrational.

By 1945, the wilder excesses of European nationalism and fascism had devalued romantic rhetoric as a political language. With the rise of the Cold War against a perceived universal Marxist challenge, eighteenth-century thinkers like Edmund Burke, that passionate but ambivalent Irish conservative, were resurrected as standard-bearers of liberal capitalism, especially by conservative American scholars, but it was only a question of time before some of the leading figures of the High Scottish Enlightenment were so used. The Moderate *literati*, despite a rhetorical technique which paraded a willingness to look at all points of view on a question, and a studied politeness and seeming moderation, were, in fact, consistent political reactionaries. They opposed virtually every politically progressive movement of their time: parliamentary reform, burgh reform, church reform, colonial rights, or repeal of the Test Act. Most of them did accept that the virtue which they preached as the necessary foundation of a healthy state could not be totally passive, though they confined its allowable activism to a manly defence of the *status quo* in a crisis. When, after 1757, it became clear that Westminster distrusted the Scots too much to allow them to have a militia like the newly reactivated English one, they were embarrassed and angry. Not so Adam Smith and David Hume. Their dilution of the heritage of 1688 had reached the stage where, though of course reluctant to admit it in so many words, they did not believe in participative liberty at all, only in equality before the law and freedom to shop around for the cheapest goods. Not much wonder that early exponents of post-1945 radical rightism like F. A. Hayek were attracted by selected thinkers of the later Scottish Enlightenment.

In the last decade, there has arisen a quasi-religious cult of Adam Smith in the hands of people who do not appear to have read even his best-known book, for it is impossible to believe that the members of the Adam Smith Institute approve of either his deep distrust of businessmen or his insistence that the weight of taxation (all, not some, taxation) should be relative to income. Selectivity within the Smith *oeuvre* is matched by the selectivity in recreating his context. Predecessors like Sir James Steuart, and formidable critics like the Eighth Earl of Lauderdale, simply vanish, as does the 'Country' Whig tradition which, from Fletcher to Lauderdale, insisted against the predominant 'Court' Whigs that passive liberty is no liberty at all. From the Revolution to the Edinburgh of the economist Lauderdale and the poet and novelist Scott, historians need to recreate the full range of contemporary debate, not least because many of the problems men wrestled with then are still with us and it is not true that there is only one solution. There were and are always alternatives.

The Making of industrial and urban society: Scotland 1780–1840

T. M. DEVINE

Professor of Modern History, Strathclyde University

As OTHER WRITERS IN THIS VOLUME have shown, Scottish society before the later eighteenth century was far from static. The commercialisation of agriculture both in the Highlands and Lowlands was advancing as proprietors began increasingly to extract more revenue from their estates to support higher standards of living. Foreign trade, especially the Atlantic sector in general and Glasgow commerce in particular, experienced precocious growth from the 1740s. The significance of urban life became greater, not simply because of the expansion of the larger burghs of Glasgow, Edinburgh and Aberdeen but also as a result of the proliferation of smaller regional and local centres. But in a structural sense, Scotland was still relatively unchanged. Such economic expansion as did occur tended to develop along existing lines: for the most part it was somewhat sluggish and the overwhelming predominance of agriculture and rural society remained. As late as 1750 probably no more than one Scot in eight was a townsman.

From the last quarter of the eighteenth century there was a significant change of gear. Economic growth not only became faster but was sustained on a broad front. One estimate suggests that the volume of grain brought to market doubled and animal products increased six-fold between 1740 and the 1820s. Exports rose ninefold from 1785 to 1835 and the relative share of manufactures in this total consistently increased. Linen output climbed from over 12 million yards in the 1770s to over 30 million yards by the early 1820s. One clear sign that Scotland was a much wealthier society as a consequence of this huge increase in production and productive capacity was its ability to absorb increasing numbers of people and to feed and employ them. Webster put Scottish population at over 1,265,000 in the 1750s. By 1801 this had risen to over 1,600,000 and by 1831 to well over 2 millions. Growth had occurred before, but this was a rate never equalled in previous periods. More importantly, it was sustained expansion which was not impeded as it had been in the past by limitations on food supply or in employment opportunities.

It is, of course, important to stress that there was no complete break with the past. By 1830 most Scots still worked in a rural environment as their ancestors had done. The governing class of the old society, the greater landowners and their kin and associates in the legal profession, still dominated despite the active criticism of the reform movements of the 1790s and during the years after the end of the Napoleonic Wars. Furthermore, industrial expansion before 1830 was narrowly based on cotton, linen and woollen textiles, and growth in coal-mining and iron production was much more sluggish. Sir John Sinclair confidently estimated that over ninety per cent of Scottish industrial workers in the early nineteenth century were occupied in the textile sector. The process of industrialisation was therefore far from complete in 1830. The great late nineteenth century staples of coal, iron, engineering and shipbuilding were all underdeveloped. Their phase of vigorous expansion lay in the future. Moreover, technical change, the substitution of machinery for human effort, was mainly confined to some of the textile, chemical and metal industries. In consequence, the factory, the classic symbol of the new age, had not yet become the characteristic working environment. Most Scots still laboured on the land, in the home, or in the workshop rather than in the new industrial complexes each employing several hundred people.

Yet, recognition of these continuities should not obscure the fundamental changes in Scottish life which took place during this period and which do suggest a major and decisive break with the past. It is true that as late as 1821 as many as two Scots in three still lived and worked on the farm, on the croft, in the country village or in the small town. However, their way of life was quite different from that of their forebears. Before the middle decades of the eighteenth century there were few entirely landless groups in the Scottish countryside. Rural tradesmen normally had a patch of land, much of the agricultural labour force was recruited from cottar families, small tenants practising subsistence husbandry proliferated in many areas, and even 'landless' farm servants were reared in peasant households before they were hired in their teenage years by larger farmers. On the very eve of the great movement towards agrarian reorganisation the vast majority of rural dwellers in Scotland depended to a greater or lesser extent on access to land. In that sense, there was a closer resemblance to the characteristic peasant societies of continental Europe than to many areas in England where the 'modern' social structure of landowners, farmers and landless labourers was already in place by the early eighteenth century.

That system was imposed on Lowland Scotland over a much shorter period of time. From the 1780s the pace of agrarian change quickened as small farms were reorganised and consolidated, fields enclosed and the subtenantry, the single most numerous class in the old world, rapidly eliminated.The process occurred with little protest and perhaps for that reason its scale and speed has not been sufficiently recognised. Over two or three generations the traditional peasant society was removed and a new rural social order which survived into the twentieth century established in its place. This was radically different from that of the past in the sense that the vast majority of those who worked in Lowland agriculture no longer depended on subsistence plots to survive but rather on their capacity to sell their labour power to employing farmers in the market place.

At first glance, the pattern in the Highlands seems to be somewhat different. The connection between the people and the land which was severed in the Lowlands was maintained in many parts in the region and above all along the western mainland and throughout the inner and outer Hebrides. There the indigenous population continued to eke out a living on crofts, smallholdings and subtenancies through a combination of potato cultivation, cattle rearing, subsistence fishing and temporary migration. Ironically, however, social change in this region was probably more traumatic and cataclysmic than anywhere in the Lowlands. The old military society, already in decline in the early eighteenth century, was replaced by an entirely new order in which the land and the population of the region were subordinated to the revenue needs of the proprietors and the huge increase in external demand from the Lowlands and England for such Highland products as kelp, fish, cattle, wool, mutton, whisky, timber and slate. These forces of commercialisation produced two major phases of Clearance. In the first period the communal farming settlements or *bailetoun* were dissolved between *c*.1730 and

1820 and replaced by a structure of individual smallholdings or crofts in which the people worked the land but also produced cash commodities for southern markets. After the end of the Napoleonic Wars, however, a collapse in kelp markets, stagnation in fishing and a slump in cattle prices ushered in the second phase of Clearance as proprietors laid down more territory for sheep farming. This led to an even more radical shift in the distribution of population, increases in eviction and an acceleration in the rate of migration and emigration. Unlike the pattern in the Lowland countryside economic change in the Highlands provoked embittered if sporadic protest and much social alienation. Yet both regions were subjected to the same fundamental pressures on social relationships and social structure: the new revenue demands of the landowners, the ideological forces of 'improvement' and, above all, the influence of burgeoning markets for food, raw materials and labour.

The principal source of this market growth was the Scottish towns and cities. Recent research has established a truly remarkable rate of urban expansion from the later eighteenth century. In 1700, Scotland was tenth in a league table of 'urbanised societies' in Europe as measured by the proportion of population living in towns of 10,000 inhabitants or above. By the 1750s it had risen to seventh and by 1800 was already one of the five most urbanised countries in western Europe, alongside England, the Netherlands, Belgium and northern Italy. But Scotland had achieved this position over a much shorter period of time. Furthermore, the process of urbanisation continued to accelerate, so that by the 1850s more Scots lived in large towns than in any other European society with the single exception of England. This was indeed a fundamental social transformation even when it is recognised that the majority of the Scottish population still remained rural dwellers. The rapidly expanding urban areas were no longer simply adjuncts to an overwhelmingly rural society as they had been in the early eighteenth century. Rather they had become the dynamic centres of economic change. The lives of people in the countryside were altered by the needs of the teeming cities for foods and raw materials and the impact these needs and the sale of their products had on the social structure of countless communities in the Highlands and Lowlands.

A number of factors help to explain this extraordinary rate of town growth. It was assisted by the changes in Scottish agriculture already surveyed which through reorganisation of farms, more efficient use of labour and improved rotations contributed to an increase in food supply which allowed the urban masses to be fed. Again, as the movement of goods and raw materials expanded, towns had to develop as centres of exchange, providing the commercial, financial and legal services now required by the market economy. Thus Perth, Haddington, Ayr, Dumfries and Stirling owed much of their growth in this period to the requirements of their rural hinterlands for such facilities. Urban development was also influenced by foreign trade. In the eighteenth century, Scotland was in a superb geographical position to exploit the changing direction of international commerce from the Mediterranean to the Atlantic. This momentous alteration in transcontinental trade was a highly dynamic factor in port development along the whole western coast of Europe from Cork to Cadiz. Scotland was virtually at the crossroads of the new system and the Clyde ports grew rapidly to become great centres for the importation of tobacco, sugar and raw cotton. It was no coincidence that in the period after 1780 four of the five fastest-growing towns in Scotland were in the Clyde basin. Greenock may be taken as the archetypal port town, expanding from a population of 2,000 in 1700 to 17,500 in 1831.

Yet, in the long run, the most critical factor was the expansion of manufacturing industry. Of the thirteen largest towns in early nineteenth century Scotland, five at least trebled their population size between c.1750 and 1821. In addition to Greenock these were Glasgow (from 31,700 to 147,000), Paisley (6,800 to 47,000), Kilmarnock (4,400 to 12,700) and Falkirk (3,900 to 11,500). Greenock apart, all these towns depended directly or indirectly on manufacturing industry. It was clearly industrial concentration in towns which set the pace of Scottish urbanisation.

But the process was not inevitable in the short run. Indeed, by the 1830s, most industrial activity was still located in the village or the small town rather than the large city and this pattern helps to explain why most Scots still lived and worked in a rural setting at that date. The water-powered cotton factories, coal mining and pig-iron manufacturers were all in the country. In the long run, however, there were obvious advantages in industrial concentration in towns; firms saved the cost of providing accommodation and other facilities for their workers from their own resources; they were also guaranteed access to a huge pool of labour; transport costs between sources of supply, finishing trades and repair shops could be markedly reduced or virtually eliminated by the close proximity of complementary economic activities. In cotton-spinning, and eventually in other textile industries, steam power encouraged industrial settlements on the coalfields and removed the one major obstacle which had previously limited the expansion of manufacturing in the large towns. Glasgow provides the most dramatic case of the pattern of change. In 1795 the city had eleven cotton-spinning complexes but rural Renfrewshire had twelve. The basic need to have secure access to water power obviously diluted Glasgow's other attractions as a potential centre of textile production. However, the adoption of steam-based technology after 1800 allowed expansion on a massive scale in the city and its immediate environs. By 1839, out of 192 cotton mills in Scotland, 98 were in or near Glasgow.

Urban growth at such speed suggests a remarkably high rate of human mobility because the towns grew primarily through inward migration. In most areas of western Europe, most people lived and died in the parishes of their birth. But in Scotland, temporary and permanent migration was the norm rather than the exception. Only 47 per cent of the inhabitants of the ten principal Scottish towns in 1851 had been born in them. The majority of migrants were young adults who had travelled relatively short distances within the Lowlands. Increasingly, however, Highland movement, especially to the western towns, became significant though it was soon quickly dwarfed by Irish immigration. Population pressure, difficulties in the Ulster linen industry and ease of access to the Clyde ports afforded by the new steamships all contributed to this. By 1841 it has been estimated that almost a quarter of the people of the western Lowlands were of Irish extraction. The majority were Catholic but a substantial minority were Ulster Protestants. The scale of the movement, indigenous Scottish anti-Catholicism and the transfer of ancient rivalries from Ireland fuelled sectarian tensions in the developing urban society.

It was primarily because of the sheer speed of urban expansion and inward migration that the larger towns steadily became more lethal in this period. The contemporary structures of sanitation and waste disposal were often simply overwhelmed in a rising tide of humanity. Scottish conditions were worse than elsewhere in Britain.

As Edwin Chadwick put it in 1842: 'There is evidence to prove that the mortality from fever is greater in Glasgow, Edinburgh and Dundee than in the most crowded towns in England.' By that decade, urban Scotland was approaching a social crisis of unprecedented proportions. Meaningful efforts at reform were constrained by contemporary ideologies which blamed poverty and squalor on weaknesses of character rather than on environmental pressures. The urban society had been born but not until the second half of the nineteenth century were its problems addressed in a serious way.

The rapid expansion of industry and the larger towns also inevitably imposed immense strain on the institutions of government. The Scottish political system was notoriously unrepresentative and dominated by the greater landed families and their associates. In 1831, one Englishman in thirty could vote, while at the same date only one Scot in six hundred was enfranchised. About three thousand 'county freeholders' voted for the thirty county members and the fifteen burgh members were elected by the oligarchic town councils. The system reflected the belief that only the small élite who possessed a great deal of property in land, those who had a major stake in the country, could be trusted to govern the country with prudence. However, as industrial and urban wealth increased, the existing political structure seemed to many to be both unjust, corrupt and anachronistic. From the later eighteenth century it was confronted by a series of challenges both from those members of the propertied classes who were outside the 'political nation' and, even more ominously, from the common people who achieved in this period a new awareness of their democratic rights.

There had been a movement for burgh reform in the 1780s and this was followed in 1792-3 by a short-lived but significant campaign for electoral reform stimulated by the French Revolution. The Societies of Friends of the People were eventually crushed by draconian government action and their leadership sentenced to transportation to Botany Bay. Not until after the Napoleonic Wars did the reform movement recover enough confidence to mount a fresh challenge. Huge public meetings, especially in the west of Scotland, the development of a radical press, the interaction between trade unions and reform groups and closer contact with English radicals culminated in the so-called 'Radical War' of 1820. Economic distress and the new political ideas of the time fused to produce a major political crisis. For several days, an estimated 50,000 in the industrial west stopped work and some groups openly carried weapons and took part in military drill. In the event, the threatened revolution did not take place and the few skirmishes which occurred were easily won by the army. Poor planning, the failure of English radicals to respond and the loyalty of the Scottish propertied classes and the military were all important factors in explaining the victory of government. But the events of 1820 were nevertheless significant in demonstrating a new if ephemeral collectivity of purpose among the working classes, the alienation of many from the existing system and the widespread popularity of democratic ideas.

All this represented a significant change from the middle decades of the eighteenth century. But the reform movements were not powerful enough to force any fundamental alteration in the political structure. Even the Reform Act of 1832 can be seen as a means of perpetuating old authority by partially extending the franchise within the propertied classes. It was not so much a resounding defeat for the existing régime as a further demonstration of its essential resilience and capacity for survival. Despite structural changes in both economy and society, Scotland in the 1830s was still dominated by the same social class who had held power in the old world. To some extent this was because many of the economic changes of the period strengthened the material foundations of landed political supremacy. Estate rentals rose in the wake of urban demand for foods, raw materials and fuel. Much industrial activity, especially in mining, metal-working and textile processing, took place in the country village or small town rather than the large city. Furthermore, there was no massive social or ideological gulf between urban and rural élites. They shared a common faith in property ownership as the best guarantee of political stability. They were both committed to the ideals of improvement and economic progress. Many landowners were in the vanguard of the process of material transformation not only as agriculturalists but also as the founders of industrial villages and as partners in banks, road and canal companies and a host of manufacturing ventures. The Scottish aristocracy may have been political conservatives but they were also economic revolutionaries who went with the grain of the developing capitalist order. The old political élite therefore demonstrated considerable flexibility in the field of economic legislation. It was the unreformed political system which presided over the removal from the statute book of such paternalistic laws as the controls on wages and prices. This not only helped to accelerate the complete dominance of market forces; it also illustrates the capacity of the traditional rulers of Scottish society to adapt to the new era and, by so doing, to perpetuate their power.

In the final analysis, however, old authority survived because no effective alliance of the unenfranchised developed to threaten it. Temporary accommodation between the middle classes and the labouring classes, as 1792–3 and 1816–19 revealed, was possible. But no enduring revolutionary combination was likely to emerge. Many middle class groups feared the threat to property implicit in democratic demands and were increasingly alarmed by the menace of popular unrest and the danger of anarchy. Ironically, the French Revolution at once stimulated bourgeois interest in reform and at the same time crystallised deep concerns about the profound social instability which might follow in the wake of radical political change. The Scottish middle classes therefore preferred to flirt with reform rather than to commit themselves to it as a basic ideal. The working classes increasingly turned to it as a means of alleviating their social and economic difficulties. But they also were split along ethnic, occupational and ideological lines. A common front was difficult to achieve and virtually impossible to maintain for long. The old political order therefore emerged from the first phase of Scottish industrialisation remarkably unscathed. The power of the landed classes had been modified but was not yet supplanted.

The Victorian Transformation

R. H. CAMPBELL
Professor Emeritus, Stirling University

THE VICTORIAN TRANSFORMATION matters because it is an important phase of Scottish history in its own right and because it has influenced perceptions and attitudes towards Scottish achievements and problems to the present. It is not too much of an exaggeration to suggest that anyone who seeks to understand what Scots think of themselves at the end of the twentieth century and of their prospects in the twenty-first should go back and examine what took place in the nineteenth. Failure to investigate the Victorian transformation gives rise to distorted images of the past and, more serious still, to distorted ideas of some of the key issues of the present. It is, however, a period about which many are singularly ill-informed. It falls in that no-man's-land beyond living memory but not sufficiently far removed to be accorded serious recognition by many historians.

The transformation changed Scotland from an agrarian and rural to an industrial and urban society. Horizons widened, intellectually as well as physically. Even the remote areas became more closely integrated to the rest of Scotland, to the other parts of the United Kingdom, and to the world as railways and steamships exploited the benefits of the steam engine which Watt had demonstrated in the previous century. Three railways across the Border in 1850 gave easier access to England and provided the greatest boost to the merging of the social and political life of Great Britain since 1707. By the end of the century the integrated railway network of central Scotland reached to distant parts: to Kyle of Lochalsh in 1897 and to Mallaig in 1901. Steam navigation grew after the success of Henry Bell's Comet in 1812. With the economy in fuel consumption which came with the compound engine in the second half of the nineteenth century long voyages by steamships became economic. A network of shipping services from Scotland was built up and Scots were behind many of the extensive commercial services which expanded throughout the world. The links which were retained with Scotland varied; some were only sentimental, others proved to be of lasting benefit. Goods, capital and people moved more freely in the later nineteenth century and this provides the key to understanding the Victorian transformation.

It is not necessary to be an economic determinist to see that the transformation was rooted in economic change. Scotland's expansion came from behind England in the eighteenth century to achieve such international prominence by the end of the nineteenth that Scotland could be described as the workshop of the Empire and without too much exaggeration as the workshop of the world. International trading was far from being new in the nineteenth century; the response was. In the eighteenth century much trade had been the carrying of goods produced and consumed elsewhere, the sugar, molasses and tobacco which were the basis of the fortunes of many Scottish merchants. By contrast, the successful trade of the nineteenth century was based on domestic industrial production. There was, however, a significant change. The origins of one group of industries, the textiles, were in the established wool and linen trades of the pre-industrial age. While they continued, with their own areas of success in the Borders and in the east of Scotland respectively, the striking growth of textiles in the early nineteenth century was in the manufacture of cotton goods – a vulnerable manufacture as it was based on an imported raw material and was dependent for a large part of its sales on overseas markets. There was a change later in the nineteenth century when the expansion of the heavy industries used the country's own resources of coal and iron ore. Though exports absorbed a large proportion of production, often in semi-manufactured form, home demand from those who processed the metal further remained substantial. There was a defect in this success. The exhaustible natural resources were not used as carefully as in other parts of the United Kingdom or on the continent. Increasing quantities of iron ore had to be imported even before the century was over as home supplies were diminishing, and in general inadequate attention was paid to the need to keep costs low for unskilled production to survive in a competitive world. Rising costs were less harmful immediately if they were offset by special skills which differentiated Scottish products from those of competitors. The skilled engineers and shipbuilders had such skills, and so they retained markets for their output in ways which were not possible for many textile manufacturers or for those who produced semi-finished products such as pig iron. The latter suffered increasingly from competition within the United Kingdom and overseas later in the century.

Steam locomotives and steamships were the most evident sign of the success of Scottish industrial skills before 1914, but similar prosperity was found wherever there was an ability to compete through design, as in the higher quality work of the Border textile industries. The international challenge to these skilled industries was to grow in the twentieth century. Retrospective comparison with other countries shows that Scotland's industrial specialization, for all its achievements in Victoria's reign, was not suited to the more scientifically based industries of the twentieth century. Even Scotland's engineering tradition was being challenged at the end of the nineteeth century as the diesel engine and the internal combustion engine held out promising prospects of lines of development towards lighter engineering production which the Scots were less fitted to follow.

Pride in industrial achievements gave the Scots a self-confidence which bred complacency, perhaps nowhere more than in the west of Scotland, where Glasgow proudly proclaimed itself as the Second City, not only demographically. The confidence was hardly surprising as Scottish-built ships and locomotives traversed the world, but the satisfaction was insecurely based. The absence of serious competition in the international economy came to an end and the pattern of world demand shifted. That contemporaries did not see what lay ahead can be understood and excused; that longer-term failure to recognise the nature of change should persist throughout much of the twentieth century is less excusable and shows how deep-seated was the complacency which arose from the very success of the Victorian industrial transformation.

Rural Scotland also changed as it moved increasingly into its subordinate role of meeting the needs of an industrial society which was part of an expanding network of world trade.The capability of doing so was determined by physical, topographical and climatic conditions, which meant that agricultural conditions within Scotland differed, often markedly, from each other and from those in other parts of the British Isles. In general, apart from some restricted areas,

Scotland was a country where livestock and not arable husbandry dominated, as in the beef cattle which moved by steamship from the north-east to meet urban demand throughout Britain, in the sheep husbandry which spread over Scottish hills, and in the dairying which flourished around the urban areas and especially in the south-west. Specialization in livestock husbandry protected Scottish agriculture from some of the effects of cheap imports of grain from overseas in the later nineteenth century. The cultivation of wheat suffered most of all but that was of little consequence in Scotland where the main grain crop was oats, which was grown not usually as a cash crop but for feeding to livestock on the farm. More important for the prosperity of much of Scottish agriculture was the growing demand within the United Kingdom for beef, milk, butter, cheese, the perishable foodstuffs which came with the adoption of a more varied diet as the standard of living rose in the populous urban districts. The adverse effects of the growing international trade in foodstuffs became more acute at the end of the century when refrigeration enabled more perishable commodities to be imported.

The tenurial structure in the Scottish countryside was stable throughout much of Victoria's reign, with tenants holding long leases, which were often broken into shorter terms as agricultural prices fell from the 1870s. Social domination by landowners was still strong in the middle of the century. The challenges which came were often spearheaded by new commercial interests in the countryside, by the grain and manure merchants, even by some successful tenant farmers, who resented any perpetuation of old privileges as political rights broadened. By the later nineteenth century many of the privileges of landownership, some of which had been increased only earlier in the century, were being abolished or watered down. Estates were being disentailed; the position of the landowner as a preferred creditor was diminished; the game laws were modified; in the early years of the twentieth century better provision for compensation for improvements by tenants was made. These were radical changes in a traditional countryside, but the political and fiscal attack on the landowners reached new heights with Liberal administrations later in the century. Death duties from 1894 and threats of taxation of land values in the budget of 1909 were the last straws for many. The major changes which were to come as estates were broken up came later when the brief period of agricultural prosperity after the end of the First World War gave the traditional proprietors the opportunity to sell. Once again the roots of change were established before the war, which, with its severe loss of life among landed families, finally removed many incentives to continue in traditional ways. The political attack succeeded; it did not recognise the longer-term consequences of success, nor have many subsequent commentators. It made way for the entrenched owner-occupier, and so closed the path of economic and social mobility which the old system of tenancy had opened for those with limited capacity but with the reputation for unlimited application.

These economic changes were linked to demographic movements which had widespread social effects. The population was almost three times as large at the end of the century as it had been at the beginning, an increase which masked an unusual feature. In the first half of the century the actual increase probably exceeded the natural increase of births over deaths; thereafter there were more emigrants than immigrants in each decade, though the net loss was always less than the natural increase. How many went to other parts of the United Kingdom or overseas is uncertain. One calculation suggests that more, especially males, went overseas. So many emigrated that Scotland had some of the highest losses in proportion to its population of any European country. So often this striking characteristic is thought to have been the outcome of movement from rural areas, particularly from the Highlands, but, unlike other countries in Europe with high levels of migration, those who left Scotland came from all over the country, from the urban as well as from the rural areas, and from industry as well as from agriculture. There is a paradox in emigration from Scotland. It was at its peak when the economy was prosperous and when many emigrants had shared in it. They were not escaping destitution but were seeking to better their condition in other parts of the United Kingdom or overseas. They were part of that increasing internationalization of population movement which came to an end in 1914.

Probably more significant in the Victorian transformation of Scotland was the changing distribution of the rising population which remained. Not all of the increase could be supported in the place of birth. The populations of three counties reached their peaks in 1831 and others followed in subsequent decades. They stretched throughout Scotland but were all rural. The industrial belt

provided a convenient destination for those who lived near it in
Argyllshire or parts of Perthshire, but in the far north and west,
where local opportunities for alternative employment were meagre
and where the population clung more tenaciously to the land and to
such standards of living as it could provide, which often meant
famine or something similar, the move, when it came, was often out
of Scotland altogether.

The demographic transformation of Victorian Scotland had, therefore, one outstanding characteristic, neglected by the romantic conception of Scotland fostered by the tourist and sporting interests
which prospered from the more affluent and the more mobile middle class in the later nineteenth century. More and more Scots were
no longer rural and agrarian in background and interest but urban
and industrial. Urbanisation grew throughout the century and was
among the highest in Europe, but urbanisation itself was dominated
by the four large cities, which had about one in three of the population of Scotland at the end of the century. The concentration was
encouraged by the Scottish custom of living in tenements. There
was some improvement later in the nineteenth century, but the den-
sity of Glasgow's population remained notoriously high. In short,
Scotland was an urban as well as an industrial society. Though large
areas had very few people in them, most Scots lived in crowded city
dwellings and their daily life and its problems were similar to those
found in industrial cities elsewhere. They were most obvious in the
incidence of disease and in the death rate. Its reduction, to which
medical reformers in Scotland made a distinguished contribution,
was a major cause of the increase in population.

When associated with poor standards of both public and personal
health, and with both cyclical and structural fluctuations in employment, the concentration of the population brought to an end any
possibility of caring for the unfortunates of society through the old
system of social provision based on the parish, where much of the
responsibility for providing the resources necessary rested with a
changing and often tense relationship between the established
church and the local landowners. The relief of the poor was affected
directly, as well as such limited medical aid as it brought, but so too
was the provision of education. In theory, but much less so in practice, the care of the established church for the material and intellectual development of its parishioners may have worked in the rural

parishes in which many Scots still lived at the beginning of the nineteenth century. Conditions were very different at its end. The problems of a growing industrial society alone would have brought to an
end the system of social provision which had survived in some form
for centuries, but the church itself experienced major changes which
left it unable to meet its old responsibilities which it was often reluctant to surrender. While the changes which came with industrialization varied between different countries more in degree than in
kind, the ecclesiastical provision and its social obligations were
unique to Scotland.

The authority of the established church had been undermined in
the eighteenth century through the growth of dissent, the strength
of which has often been underestimated by the undue prominence
given to the established church in much historical writing. The variety of ecclesiastical affiliations and of theological opinion is masked
still further when changes in the establishment are portrayed as a
clear-cut move from domination by the Moderates, the products of
the enlightened eighteenth century, to domination by the more
evangelical Popular party as the latter gained ground from the early
years of the nineteenth century. Such an unequivocal distinction is
usually dependent on the evidence of what took place at the General
Assembly. It concentrates on the issue of patronage, on whether the
parish minister should be appointed by the patron or by the congregation. On other matters, and generally at parochial level, the distinction between the two points of view was not so clear and the
diversity of opinions was such that a division into two parties is a
questionable simplification. Since the evaluation of what took place
is usually based on the writings, speeches and sermons of a narrow
range of clerical opinion, or on the contributions of a few, highly
unusual lawyers, the events of those years, so central to much
Scottish history, hardly give a clear interpretation of what the lay-
man, and even more so the laywoman, thought about what was hap-
pening. Presbyterianism in Scotland was clerically dominated in
spite of claims to the contrary.

It was, however, on the issue of patronage that dissent from the
establishment had grown in the eighteenth century and it disrupted
the established church in 1843. The Disruption had repercussions in
Scottish life throughout the nineteenth century (not only in religious affairs); shortly after this major fracture, however, presbyteri-

anism in Scotland saw moves towards a degree of reunification with the consolidation of several of the earlier dissenting traditions into the United Presbyterian Church in 1847. It represented the old voluntary standpoint which had opposed the state connection of the establishment, so providing a barrier to unity with the Free Church until the latter had itself moved substantially in that direction in the course of its opposition to the establishment. It was the end of the century, in 1900, before the United Presbyterian and the Free Churches merged to form the United Free Church, leaving minor groupings of the Free Presbyterians and the Continuing Free Church on the way. Though the move towards greater organisational unity in the second half of the nineteenth century was a marked contrast from the experience of the first half, it was not an age of unsullied brotherly love. The bitterness of the dispute after 1843 continued and was especially acute whenever the establishment tried to retain its influence and privileges although an increasing number of Scots, even of presbyterian Scots, were outwith its fold. Allegiances varied geographically. The establishment, always linked to landowners, even though many were not of its communion, retained its place in rural areas, though not in the Highlands, while the Free Church and the United Presbyterian Church gained their most influential support from the urban middle class, a support which was to be reflected in differing political allegiances. The result was mixed. Rivalry between denominations, especially between the Free Church and the establishment, did more than provide a proliferation of church buildings, especially for the more affluent adherents, an impressive activity which has certainly mattered to later generations, plagued as they are with the maintenance of costly surplus buildings and the readjustment of dwindling congregations in areas of gross overprovision. Their rivalry absorbed much attention in Scottish life in the late nineteenth century and conditioned approaches to many secular problems by influential groups.The less influential, and the less affluent, especially in the towns, were never overwhelming supporters of any denomination. Church attendance was not as universal as is sometimes claimed.

Church history in Scotland has suffered from undue attention being given to the establishment and to disputes over church order and from too little attention to what people believed. In many cases belief was probably minimal and church affiliation a matter of mere convention, or a sign of social standing, which was made more effective through election to the eldership, and useful because of the influence the established church and the mainline denominations had generally in society, even as they became alienated from many. The nineteenth century saw major transformations in theological outlook, two in particular, originating outside Scotland. The two were the growth of theological liberalism arising from biblical criticism and, by contrast, the growth of evangelistic fervour associated with the missions of Moody and Sankey. The immediate influence of the first was confined to rarefied academic circles but through charges and rebuttals of heresy at the highest levels led in practice to the rejection of some of the old confessional standards of the presbyterian churches. The second was more widely influential but, as some of its most ardent supporters were in lower social classes, its effects have been ignored in so much church historiography For the same reason a more direct challenge to the domination of traditional presbyterianism has often been neglected until its scale meant that it could no longer be ignored. It was the growth of Roman Catholicism, a growth which was only one aspect of the arrival of large numbers of Irish immigrants, many of whom were strongly Protestant in any case, and which contributed to the cultural transformation of the urban areas, most of all in the west. The reestablishment of the hierarchy in 1878 was symptomatic of the change and heralded the beginning of the end of Protestant, which in Scotland meant presbyterian, domination, though the change was not accepted until well after the end of the nineteenth century. The acceptance by presbyterians, and by the Church of Scotland in particular, that they alone mattered ecclesiastically, and so in many walks of life, was an attitude not easily dislodged.

Ecclesiastical wrangling itself ensured that the social provision of the old rural society under the control of a largely united church could continue no longer. The poor law came under new forms of secular control in 1845 but major intervention by the state in education was delayed until 1872, partly because the Free Church provided a notable increase in accommodation and was always suspicious of any changes which might have left the establishment with a measure of privilege in a more secular framework. The intervention which came after 1872 was directed as much to ensuring more regular attendance for primary education as to providing better and more advanced facilities.

In the universities investigations by reforming liberals from the 1830s removed many privileges under which, though this was not recognized by the reformers, the universities had achieved international distinction in the previous century. The changes were less marked in organization than in the pressure to move from a more general education to greater specialization. Some modern writers have taken the changes to be evidence of anglicizing influences, usually to be deplored. Greater specialization had repercussions on open entry and made recruitment from a wide variety of social classes and schools more difficult. The change was less than is sometimes implied. The openness in the past never led in practice to a substantial number of students coming from the less well-off sections of society. The move towards greater specialization was caused by much more fundamental reasons than any increased anglicizing influence, reasons which Scottish education could ignore only at its peril in the world of the later nineteenth century. Greater specialization was needed to meet the needs of those who aspired to professional training, which was becoming more specialized itself, and so was sought after by the Scottish commercial and professional classes whose needs determined the pattern of education. The direction of professional training in Scotland itself may have been misguided or deficient. Some critics thought scientific endeavour was poor and suffered from a reluctance to provide the resources needed for higher achievement; there were also differences of opinion on the direction progress should take, whether it should be more practical and less abstract or not. However, one characteristic of the later nineteenth century is clear. Scottish education was not closely allied with industrial activities, a combination which had been so conspicuously successful in the eighteenth century and which was becoming more and more successful in some continental countries which were also becoming Scotland's industrial competitors. The future lay less in success in the empirical approach to mechanical engineering, which had been behind so much Scottish industrial success, and more in the mathematical basis of much modern science where the Scots were deficient. Retention of the old broadly-based education, with its philosophical bias, which it has become fashionable to admire, would not have reduced the deficiency. It would have confirmed it.

The state was kept out of much intervention in the problems of society not only by ecclesiastical wrangling; the political scene itself was not encouraging. Scotland was overwhelmingly Liberal from 1832, a political affiliation which was given an impetus by the association of their landowning opponents with the Conservatives in the minds of many in the Free Church and by the attractions of Gladstonian moral fervour. There was a tradition of individualism and self-help throughout Scotland, so that the respectable working class was as keen as the middle class to maintain its values and distinctive way of life against the undeserving poor. This tradition, and any perceived perpetuation of it to more modern times, need to be treated with some qualification. The roots of the challenge to it are to be found in the Victorian transformation. The highly localized administration of such rudimentary social services as existed was passing from parochial authorities to higher bodies, even as the church gave way to secular intervention within them. From 1845 the Board of Supervision encouraged a common pattern of relief of the poor, even if it did not direct its adoption rigidly until it was superseded by the Local Government Board in 1894; the Scotch Education Department came into existence in 1872 as the state took over responsibility for education; and the county administration assumed a more recognizably twentieth-century look in 1889 when the new county councils took over the responsibilites which had been added piecemeal to the old Commissioners of Supply. In some form or other the state was taking an interest in, and a responsibility for, provision in an increased range of public services. It was a challenge to the old liberal individualism, but it was not reflected significantly in any challenge to the political Liberal domination. Until the twentieth century there was little support for the challenges from socialism or from any form of Scottish independence movement. Indeed the latter, in a variety of manifestations, tended to be the preserve of those who still maintained the old values of liberal individualism. Scottish liberalism was, however, split by the proposals for Irish home rule. The Ulster Protestant connection was strong and so Liberal Unionism gained a hold in the west of Scotland, a hold which was to persist until the twentieth century. Politically the Victorian transformation saw the Scots content with a United Kingdom. Its economic advantages were too great and too obvious for many to doubt its political desirability.

The nature of these political issues, which were to become more acute in the twentieth century, can be understood only through the Victorian transformation which prepared the way for them. The root of the problem is the frequent failure to recognize how unique and how transient were the achievements of the transformation. The achievements were largely a response to a set of peculiarly favourable external circumstances and not a response which rested entirely on indigenous Scottish ability. The most fundamental favourable circumstance was the external one of the expanding international economy. From its opportunities, challenges and disciplines there was not, and never can be, any escape for a country which seeks a high standard of living. The Empire made the penetration of the international economy a little easier but not much, and to stress it as the crucial determinant of Scottish success is misleading. The key factor was an open trading system world wide in which there was little competition, and where expansion to the less well-developed parts offset the difficulties of competition in the more developed when it arose. Complementing the external opportunities were the favourable internal endowments of coal and iron ore which were at the base of so much of the successful economic expansion of the century. Bringing them together, however, was the achievement of able entrepreneurs, who had a zest for profits in the market economy. It was in that field, so often decried by modern commentators, in an age when the Scots were not abashed at trying to make money and saw no need to apologize for doing so, that there was truly indigenous achievement. It is seen in the origins of Scottish entrepreneurs in many fields. It was, however, a narrow and passing basis for continuing economic success.

Failure to recognise both the source of the strength of the success and the corresponding weakness behind the Victorian transformation has had long-term consequences which matter. It has given rise to unrealistic, even to misleading assessments of Scotland's place and prospects in the late twentieth century. The economic success of the nineteenth century was bound to come to an end unless the internal response consistently measured up to the opportunities available in an international economy in which the pace of change was accelerating and of which Scotland was part. The Victorian transformation did not prepare the Scots well to meet this challenge of later years. In much of the nineteenth century it was possible to succeed with a limited internal response because external conditions were favourable and so the popular conception of the independent, enterprising Scot providing the key to the achievements of the nineteenth century is something of a myth. The Scots were simply fortunate; they never had it so easy again as in the nineteenth century. However, a belief that it was otherwise inculcated a complacent confidence in their superiority, and this is not easily dislodged; it encourages self-satisfied basking in past glories and correspondingly to the belief that later achievements are underestimated: so, above all, any later lack of success must be the fault of some malevolent force or being. In the late twentieth century, with its commonly-held assumption that remedies lie in collective action, it is easy to believe that the cure is possible with political changes of some kind. Looking back, however, the most striking change since Victoria's day is not that there has come a relative decline in the international economic standing of Scotland, which was bound to happen, but that the Scots themselves show less ability to exploit such opportunities as are available than they once did. An impressive contrast between the nineteenth and the twentieth centuries is that the race of successful Victorian entrepreneurs has not been replaced. However, their zest for profits in the international economy has been replaced by the rejection of their culture of success, and by the adoption of a high moral tone in doing so, with little recognition of how essential it was to the vast and continuing improvement in the social welfare of all Scots to the present. A study of the transformation shows that the Victorians and their beliefs are still necessary to meet the demands of an ever-changing international economy. The failures of the present may spring from the rejection of some of the less conventionally-lauded Victorian values.

Modern Scotland: Remembering the People

CHRISTOPHER HARVIE

Professor of British Studies, Tübingen University

I

IN THE FIRST VERSION OF THIS ESSAY, I found myself writing something close to autobiography, which some regarded as stimulating, and others as pretentious. I was trying to make the point that contemporary Scottish history itself was subverting the fundamental framework for understanding that I and my generation had accepted at university of Scotland as a regional variation on a 'British' norm and that this framework had yet to be replaced by an interpretive structure which was objectively more satisfactory. In this situation, the 'theoretical history' of the intellectual autobiography such as Carlyle and Hugh Miller had written in the equally turbulent nineteenth century seemed a more fruitful approach. This was in 1990, and was probably a bit out of date even then.

I began by recollecting Winston Smith's toast 'to the past!' in *1984*: a plea for truth in language and history, when both were endangered. If Orwell had observed a language, Gaelic, retreating like English under the pressure of Oceania's Newspeak, the Scottish past seemed under threat from a government which held to a policy of centralization, abetted by a spineless Scottish Office. Despite an energetic Scottish cultural revival in the 1980s, the drive to a United Kingdom school curriculum seemed an implicit threat. Could a premier doubtful about the idea of society accept any social *rationale* for historical study? Mrs Thatcher's sensitivity about British sovereignty in a federalized Europe made her attempt to dig a moat defensive against any 'Europe of the Regions', making Scotland a prime target for tidying-up. Kenneth Baker as Secretary of State for Education [in England and Wales] seemed to want a sort of Anglo-Gaullist history, embalming the image of Britain as 'progressive'; he was suspicious of notions of 'empathy' in historical teaching, or of history as techniques and tools, and preferred a version of the story of our

nation akin to the 'history of the regiment' that soldiers are subjected to. Thatcherism would fight for centralism and turn choice parts
of the archaic social and material fabric into marketable 'heritage'.
Within a fortnight of the submission of my manuscript, Thatcher
fell, fulminating in her memoirs against educational 'progressives'
and Scots alike. Thereafter it was Anglocentric history which
became pathological. In the hands of the Conservative right –
Jonathan Clark, Corelli Barnett, Andrew Roberts or John Charmley
– it turned in on itself, became an autopsy of iconic careers once
revered but now seen as problematic, and of once-great institutions
of state. On the Charter 88 centre-left the monarchy, popular patriotism and the English gentleman were now regarded as signs of
national decline, but within misty and debatable formulations of
'Englishness'. In Scotland the tide has set in the other direction.
After stripping away tartanry and Jacobite sentimentalism, definitions of 'Scottishness' are fairly precise; the task is to get at the fac-
tual record and fill up its lacunae. Multi-national London media
churn out their ever-profitable nostalgic romanticism but now focus
this through the proscenium of British backwardness. (A German
friend helpfully described the Merchant-Ivory adaptation of E. M.
Forster's *Maurice* as 'a coffee-table film'.)The civic responsibilities
which goad research in Scotland are lacking down south, partly
because of centralization and the imperial legacy, but more because
of the sheer commercialism of the metropolis. Decline has become
box-office. In my first revision of *No Gods and Precious Few Heroes*
in 1987 I found that not only had many of the gaps in the twentieth-
century account been filled up between 1981 and 1986, but that
most of these studies had been published *in* Scotland. Thus the story
that the Scots have been telling each other is much more enterprising, exploratory and critical: history in Collingwood's sense of
discovering the questions which people in the past had been asking
about their society.

II
BY 1990 IN FACT IT WAS POSSIBLE to realize that the old 'formal' curriculum was itself ideology, and fairly unhelpful to the issues beset-
ting us. We were fed on nineteenth-century notions of benign evolution of national unity – Italy, the United States and (somewhat less
commendable but still *inevitable*) Germany. British homogeneity

was simply assumed and we were too polite to go on about it. Marxists, too, regarded this as natural: parliamentary sovereignty went hand-in-hand with capitalist rationality. Where Goethe talked of Walter Scott as Scottish, to Georg Lukacs he was English. Studies of the great twentieth century discontinuities – war and revolution – seemed further to emphasize UK unity and make Scottish history into the echo of an old song. Europeanization and the politics of Scotland-the-Euro-Region have eroded these simplicities, not by inflating the parochial element in Scotland – although that would have been natural enough, in the recoil against its neglect – but in pointing out the extent to which the Scottish experience relates to that of other regions and to supra-regional developments in the spheres of economics, technology, ecology and cultural history. It is the English paradigm which is eccentric and – given the UK's less than brilliant economic performance – peculiarly uninstructive. Do they 'do it better there'?

The *stasis* among conservative British historians is parallelled by the German *Historikerstreit* caused by rightists who want to 'relativize' Nazi atrocities by calibrating them in a scale determined by the excesses of the Russians and Japanese. This obscures the much more widespread movement of creating detailed local accounts of people's own experience, through labour history, local history, and 'history-workshop'-type approaches. In Tübingen this trend is exemplified by the work of the Uhland Institute for Empirical Cultural Research – whose projects (usually ending up with an exhibition and detailed catalogue) include the development of public demonstrations in industrial Germany, death and burial rituals in the South-West, the life of the workers in a university town, and (particularly valuable for comparisons with Scotland) the commercialization of rural sentimentality in the late nineteenth century. Here you can see that regional studies are not parochial but can radically enhance individual and mutual understanding. The 1990s have seen necessary international networks of communication being constructed. These seem far more important, and far less dangerous, than the implausible rebuilding of the 'political history' of the Bismarckian nation-state.

III

WHAT OUGHT THE CONCERNS OF HISTORY TO BE? The point was put to
me bluntly by a Glasgow teacher: 'How do I interest a kid in history who lives in Castlemilk?' I did my usual approach, suggesting
stimulating an interest in locality, family, work. 'There isn't anything
historical in Castlemilk, and it goes on for miles. His mother's probably a single parent.   His grandparents live miles away.
Unemployment's over fifty per cent.'   This teacher found that the
kids were most interested by a project on Mary Queen of Scots: that
the sheer unusualness of sixteenth-century Scotland, its distance
from Castlemilk, took hold of them in a way that contemporary history, at that stage, could not.   We should never underestimate the
hunger for experience, and the role that history can play in this.
Overstress it and you end up with the 'drum and trumpet' again, dis-
turbingly present in Tinseltown's recent rediscovery of Caledonia
Stern and Wild. History as pageant, the imaginative heart of our particular heartless world, all too often means the fossilized remains of
macho insensitivity and sectarian acrimony.   After Castlemilk,
where is 'history as citizenship', made so much of by Tom Johnston?
Justifying to the Castlemilk kid the raw deal he or she's been given
seems ethically dubious. But it is better than that anomie which,
through vandalism, drugs and petty crime, pushes borderline areas
under. As Andrew MacPherson has written, the 'establishment ideology' of Scottish education is firmly rooted in the Johnstonian
Gemeinschaft of the small burgh and the local all-ability secondary
school, without much of a feel for urban deprivation. In such circumstances, history has to stimulate, to generate the sort of imaginative responses which will change political relationships.   This
means resources, good teachers, and adequate back-up, retraining,
out-of-school activities: priorities and preferential treatment. Other
areas of the country, in the smaller burghs and landward districts
have, on the whole, a much better developed plateau from which to
start. They don't require didactics so much as the co-ordination of
library and information services. We now, potentially, have the sort
of equipment which enables us to swap resources around and con-
centrate them where they're needed most: encouraging history as a
central aspect of social orientation, equipping people to understand
and so change their situation. The cumulative effect of unequal

life-chances has radically disadvantaged far too many in our society, and this can only be remedied by a straegic increase of the 'guided' element in teaching: or simply *good* teaching.

IV

HISTORY IS AS MUCH A MATTER of the personality and background of the writer as of objective investigation into historical fact. My own primary induction into Scottish history fixed for me the enduring elements (typical of my generation) which were to counter-balance the orthodox 'British-history' outlook. I was, as a schoolmaster's son in the Borders, reared on oral, written and broadcast history, since my father made a lot of use of schools broadcasts and their well-produced booklets. The teaching at Kelso High School of Lewis Lawson stressed that history and geography should start with the local and knowable and then move out in a comparative way to embrace Britain, Europe and the world. Lawson conveyed an amazing amount of information and techniques: studying monasticism through the Abbey, the mediaeval town through the excavation of Roxburgh, eighteenth-century civil engineering through Rennie's Kelso and Waterloo Bridges. We learnt how to reconstruct buildings, draw historical maps, get the *Statistical Account* for information. Only now can I see in all this the ideas of John Grierson and Patrick Geddes: a democratic regionalism sidelined in favour of Great British themes.

At Royal High the exam curriculum discounted the importance of Scotland: of my teachers Bobo Aitken had been treasurer of the Scottish National Party, and Hector MacIver was a link to the literary renaissance of the 1930s. But the connections behind their approaches were only apparent long after I had finished my post-graduate work.

At Edinburgh University I didn't read Scottish History but my time of study there coincided both with the revival of labour history in the hands of John Simpson and Iain MacDougall, and the influence of four Cambridge-educated academics: Geoffrey Best, Harry Hanham, Victor Kiernan and James Cornford. The peculiarities of Scottish politics and urban organization, hitherto little explored, seemed to them so far from the English norm as to warrant research programmes. Although my own work was on the liberal movement at the old English universities, it had links with the Scottish tradition both through the careers of men such as James Bryce and through George Davie's work on the politics and philosophy of the Scottish universities. By 1969 the national revival was on us, and I was down south working for the Open University; but the germ had been planted both of new agendas – women's history, sport history, family history, the history of emigrants, immigrants and minorities – and of new techniques.

At one level the Open University, with Jennie Lee, Walter Perry, Graham Martin and Arthur Marwick, was perhaps the last attempt at a centralized 'Great British' institution. Yet, in spite of this 'Ukanian' beginning, our techniques in history teaching tried to use such new technology as TV, films, radio and radio-vision, audio and video-cassettes. We tried to take regional differentials into account. (Glasgow and the transport industries was the case study in the first Arts Foundation Course.) We aimed at equipping students to do detailed research in local history in the units of the Second Level course on *The Age of Revolutions*, dealing with the Industrial Revolution, and in the research-based senior honours course *Sources and Themes in British History 1790-1950*. They were encouraged to work largely on their own, and produced some remarkable research projects – even a Lord Provost (John Mackay, of Edinburgh) with a PhD thesis on the social history of the West Lothian shale mining area. The Open University in fact turned out to be deeply subversive of 'Britishness', stressing instead the distinctiveness of the civil societies and political traditions of the four nations. By the time I came to write *No Gods* in the late 1970s , 'homogeneity' seemed contingent on specific events, not a law of existence.

V

CURRENT SCOTTISH SOCIAL AND POLITICAL development doesn't encourage 'British' historical perspectives, but if the present government has gone soft on 'Britishness' (which didn't figure at all in its 1992 document *Scotland in the Union*) Scottish distinctiveness has been an irregular component in the past century. We have to explain why, while the autonomy of Scottish business has drastically declined, and Scots habits and dialects have been diluted by the agencies of mass-culture, home rule seems imminent, and the prospect of Scotland in a new Europe of the culture-nations gives a purpose to the nation largely lacking in the two centuries since the

Enlightenment.

By contrast, Scottish identity at the beginning of the century was politically unspecific. Although touchy nationalist bodies agitated, and the Liberals periodically passed home-rule motions, industrialists and bankers thought in terms of a world economy – measured in terms of heavy industry – and their most coherent opponents, the ethical socialists of the Independent Labour Party, thought about the brotherhood of man. The stuff of nationalism was provided by dialect, by a history preserved in ballads and popular literature, and by religious loyalties that no-one in England could be expected to fathom. This was beefed up by a distinctive urban life in tiny tenement flats, hard liquor, anti-Catholicism, and poor health conditions – partly self-inflicted.

In all of this Scotland's relations with the rest of Britain were much more conditional than they appeared (say) thirty years ago, when viewed through the 'frame' of two world wars which stressed the coherence of the United Kingdom. There was an agenda of politics which was local and preoccupied with specific Scottish concerns: religion, municipal improvement, landlord-tenant relationships; even the confrontations between the owners and the workers in industry were often settled by local trade unions and local negotiations. On top of this were two things: a socio-economic 'Atlantic arc' of city-regions interpenetrated by the transport industries and migrating capital and labour, not just Cardiff, Dublin, Liverpool, Belfast and Glasgow, but their partners in seaborne trade, whether Barcelona or Chicago. The second was an essentially British 'high politics', which the Scots tended to participate in as a high-minded fan-club, without having a deep involvement in the actual outcome of the controversies like the Eastern Question or Irish Home Rule. But even at this stage the impact of collective intervention was altering the administrative structure of politics, the restoration of the Secretaryship in 1885 being a means of arbitrating extensions of social welfare and infrastructural improvement which proved confrontational in England. This meant that education, a bugbear of religious controversy in the mid-19th century, was settled amicably in Scotland, while in England and Wales it provided the major set-to of the 1905-06 parliament. On the other hand, the initiatives after 1906 of the Liberal Secretary in agriculture and housing promised a major – and specifically Scottish – confrontation with the propertied classes.

World War I was a common experience of huge dimensions for the British people, vitiated by the incompetence of the élite in its handling of Irish affairs which led to the virtual secession of Ireland in 1921. The result of this was both a right-wing tendency in inter-war politics and a general neglect by an English-dominated parliament of the problems of the other nations of the British Isles – something enhanced by the relative reduction in Scotland's importance in terms of population and in the utility of its industries, and the terrifying dimensions of its social problems, highlighted by the 1917 report of the Royal Commission on Scottish housing. The *ethos* of the United Kingdom had been, before World War I, that 'progress' was to be found in the north and west. In the 1920s, and even more in the 1930s, the north was a problem: something registered in manufacturing and infrastructural disinvestment and even in the semantics of politics: 'derelict areas' became 'depressed areas' and finally, in 1933 – when parliament made its first initiative in regional development – 'special areas'.

The Scottish response to these problems was complex but distinctive. Despite the remarkable literary revival of the 1920s and 1930s – MacDiarmid, Muir, Gunn, Grassic Gibbon – political nationalism was never electorally successful, either as the National Party of Scotland (1928-34) or as the Scottish National Party (1934-). This period in politics has now been well documented, but we still don't know enough about why the Labour Party failed to sustain the remarkable impact that it made in 1922-24, when it displaced and all but destroyed the historic rulers of Scotland, the Liberals – nor about how the 'interventionist' ethos was created which linked industrialists, local authority chiefs, trade unionists, politicians and bureaucrats in a structure of patriotic 'proto-quangoes'. In the 1930s the foundations were laid, by Tory politicians such as Walter Elliot and Labour leaders like Sir Patrick Dollan and the Scottish Trade Union Council's William Elger, of a semi-autonomous Scottish administrative state, the beginning of regional planning, and local authority dominance in housing and education. By 1939, in the proposals of the Scottish Economic Committee and other bodies, it seemed that a distinctively Scottish approach to economic planning and industrial diversification might become a reality.

World War II saw the domestic politics of the country fall into the hands of a remarkable left-nationalist figure, Tom Johnston, still revered as the greatest-ever Secretary of State, for his initiatives in bringing hydro-power to the Scottish Highlands and setting up cross-party bodies like the Scottish Council: Development and Industry. Johnston skilfully managed a persistent level of Scottish discontent to get his administrative-devolutionist way, yet the war demanded far greater co-ordination at a British level than in 1914–18. (Scotland's role as the physical junction of Allied logistics, serving both the preparations for the Second Front and the supply of *matériel* to Russia has yet to be explored) After victory, Scotland's integration into the United Kingdom economy continued, accelerated both by the Labour government's nationalization programme and by a revival in the heavy industries which restored an almost Edwardian prosperity. Nationalism – whether amassing signatures for John MacCormick's Covenant or snatching the Stone of Destiny – seemed picturesque but irrelevant.

In the 1950s Scottish politics apparently conformed to British norms. A Unionist (rather than Conservative) establishment, protestant and generally collectivist in outlook, coexisted with Labour's control of the major cities; its extension of the public sector through housing policy led to the elimination of the private landlord. It was only when the heavy industries lapsed into a terminal decline in the late 1950s and 1960s that the institutional reform agenda of the 1930s again emerged, along with the revival of the Scottish National Party.

Since 1966 themes of economic and social change have been supplemented by political manoeuvres in which the traditional parties responded to new challenges and in so doing drifted further and further from British norms. The Conservatives first tried to recast their traditional support for decentralization into legislative devolution, but were penalized by the decay in autonomous Scottish industrial capital, and slipped further electorally. The Scottish National Party fell back from its peak in 1968, but revived in the two elections of 1974 by exploiting the issue of North Sea oil. Labour, deeply hostile to Scottish self-government, became an unwilling convert under pressure from London and articulate Scottish left-wingers like Gordon Brown, himself a historian, but failed to convert its defeat of the Scottish National Party into successful decentralization.

The failure of the devolution referendum on 1st March 1979

marks a watershed. The Conservatives abandoned the hope of a major revival and imposed a quasi-colonial form of government; for the first time a commitment to national autonomy in Scotland became general among the other parties. Mrs Thatcher's monetarist spasm in 1979-81 reacted on an already-appreciating petro-pound to throttle exports and cause numerous industrial closures. Later, in 1985-86, a takeover mania transferred two-thirds of Scottish manufacturing capital south. Was this a beneficent change in the direction of a 'post-industrial' service-industry-based society, the future projected by 'Glasgow, City of Culture'? Or was it a weakening of Scotland into a region whose resources were exploited by multinational concerns while her manufactures decayed? Would Scotland's huge natural resources of energy – oil, coal, wind and wave-power – set her up as a model region in the new Europe, and make space for a 'new' politics of sexual equality, environmental consciousness, and a commitment to world development, or would she persist as a remote and disregarded part of European geography? Home rule is Item One on the agenda of Tony Blair (educated *in* but not *by* Scotland) yet figured nowhere in the constitutional section of his recent Fabian Society 'Let Us Face the Future' lecture. We wait . . .

VI

HISTORY IS IDEOLOGY; it is also organization and experience. This is broadly the tale as I read it, and exploring it twenty years ago involved setting up new networks of sources, contacts and techniques. *No Gods and Precious Few Heroes* helped others, I hope, to construct their own narratives: expanding research and teaching to generate a history which is interesting, profitable (if need be), and civic-oriented. In the remarkable revival of art and literature that Scotland has seen since 1979, history has been, like Rilke's God, 'many thousand times present': in the plays of John McGrath, the novels of Alasdair Gray, the paintings of Ken Currie and Alan Howson, the broadcasts of Billy Kay, and the cultural criticism of Cairns Craig, Robert Crawford, Craig Beveridge and Ronnie Turnbull. For a discipline which has borne the full brunt of a government policy of throttling the humanities, the output of Scottish historians has been energetic and combative. Scotland performs well against any other European community of comparable size. (I think it does far better than Baden-Württemberg, twice its size as regards social and economic history.) Jenny Wormald's management of the *New History of Scotland* has been followed by Tom Devine and his colleagues' *People and Society in Scotland*, and Cairns Craig's *The History of Scottish Literature*, and these are only the major joint productions. It would be offensive to name the writers who have contributed effectively to filling up the *lacunae* in Scottish twentieth century history: too many good ones would get left out, and the number of turkeys is fairly insignificant. Even Gerald Warner's awful *History of the Scottish Tory Party* (published, significantly, by an impressive London house), is outweighed by his fellow Tory Michael Fry's *Patronage and Principle*, a study of Scottish politics of great critical merit. That this comes from a journalist is itself significant; rigorous historical methods have effectively been disseminated from the universities to general discourse. The sort of slap-dash 'literary' treatments (company history, political biographies) so prevalent even in the 1950s are no longer taken seriously.

Much remains to be done, not least to document the helter-skelter pace of social change since the 1960s. I am reminded of one piece of primary source material: a photograph showing a young John Mackintosh trying to hit someone much larger, during a riot in Edinburgh University's Old Quad over the invasion of Suez in October 1956. Mackintosh's death, aged only 48, seems to have occurred only the other day, but when that photo was taken the EEC had not been set up, computers were unknown, much of Africa was painted red, fridges were rare, the pill was undeveloped, and most households were without phones or cars, many without baths. In most respects Scotland in 1956 was closer to Scotland in 1914 than to the situation today, and the road from there to here *is* history.

Where do our priorities lie? A British 'national history' is of secondary importance to a history which (a) establishes the evolution of the major problems of the present, all of which, technology, communications, economics, ecology, are supra-national in character; and (b) enables people to situate themselves in a society and a *polis*. British history has its place, but it is not a dominant one, and is likely in future to become even less so. Our plea should not therefore be for some sort of quota to be devoted to Scottish history but for a rethinking of the whole curriculum which establishes real historical priorities for a European country which contributed so much to the continent's past, and can contribute so much more to its future.

Suggestions for further reading

There are two well-established series of histories of Scotland. The older is the Edinburgh History in four volumes, all published by Oliver and Boyd in Edinburgh and reissued in 1978. These are A. A. M. Duncan, *Scotland: the Making of the Kingdom* (1975); Ranald Nicholson, *Scotland: the Later Middle Ages* (1974); Gordon Donaldson, *Scotland: James V – VII* (1965) and W. Ferguson, *Scotland: 1689 to the Present* (1968). The later series, the New History of Scotland, published by Arnold in London and now being reprinted, consists of Alfred P. Smyth, *Warlords and Holy Men: Scotland AD 80–1000* (1984); G. W. S. Barrow, *Kingship and Unity: Scotland 1000–1306* (1981); Alexander Grant, *Independence and Nationhood: Scotland 1306–1469* (1984); Jenny Wormald, *Court, King and Community: Scotland 1470–1625* (1981); Rosalind Mitchison, *Lordship to Patronage: Scotland 1603–1745* (1983); Bruce Lenman, *Integration, Enlightenment and Industrialization: Scotland 1746–1832* (1981); Sidney and Olive Checkland, *Industry and Ethos: Scotland 1832–1914* (1984); Christopher Harvie, *No Gods and Precious Few Heroes: Scotland 1914–1980* (1981). Both series are equipped with full bibliographies. There is also a new, single-volume history of Scotland, Michael Lynch, *Scotland: a New History* (London 1991) in addition to Rosalind Mitchison, *A History of Scotland* (London 1982). *The Scottish Historical Review* of April 1994 gives the papers of a conference on the current state of Scottish history.

For more detailed study of the medieval period there are:
P. H. SAWYER, *The Age of the Vikings* (London 1971).
G. W. S. BARROW, *The Anglo-Norman Era in Scottish History* (Oxford 1980)
G. W. S. BARROW, *Robert the Bruce and the Community of the Realm*, (Edinburgh 1988)
LESLIE MACFARLANE *William Elphinstone and the Kingdom of Scotland, 1431– 1514* (Aberdeen 1981)
NORMAN MACDOUGALL, *James IV* (Edinburgh 1989)

Cultural and religious developments can be studied in:
I. B. COWAN, *The Scottish Reformation* (London 1982)
D. McROBERTS (ed.), *Essays on the Scottish Reformation* (Glasgow 1982)
R. D. S. JACK(ed.), *History of Scottish Literature* vol 1 (Aberdeen 1988)
A. J. MILL, *Medieval Plays in Scotland* (Edinburgh 1927)
H. SHIRE, *Song, Dance and Poetry of the Court of Scotland under James VI* (Cambridge 1969)

M. LEE, *Great Britain's Solomon: James VI and I and his Three Kingdoms*
        (Chicago 1990)
A. A. MACDONALD,M LYNCH and I. B. COWAN (eds.), *The Renaissance in
        Scotland* (Leiden 1990)
C. EDINGTON, *Court and Culture in Renaissance Scotland* (Edinburgh 1994)

For the early modern period:
T. I. RAE *The Union of 1707: its impact on Scotland* (Glasgow 1974)
P. H. SCOTT, *1707: the Union of Scotland and England* (Edinburgh 1978)
DAVID STEVENSON'S two books on the 17th-century Scottish Revolution: *The
        Scottish Revolution 1637–1644: the Triumph of the Covenanters*
        (Newton Abbot 1973), and *Revolution and Counter-Revolution in
        Scotland 1644–1653* (London 1977)
T. C. SMOUT, *A History of the Scottish People 1560–1830* (London 1969)
JOHN S. GIBSON, *Playing the Scottish Card* (Edinburgh 1988)
BRUCE P. LENMAN, *The Jacobite Cause* (Glasgow 1986)
ANAND C. CHITNIS *The Scottish Enlightenment: a Social History* (London
        1976)
R. H. CAMPBELL and ANDREW S. SINCLAIR (eds.), *The Origins and Nature of
        the Scottish Enlightenment* (Edinburgh 1982)
G. E. DAVIE, *The Scottish Enlightenment* (London 1981)
BRUCE P. LENMAN, *An Economic History of Modern Scotland 1660–1978*
        (London 1977)
R. H. CAMPBELL, *Scotland since 1707: the rise of an Industrial Society*
        (Edinburgh [2nd ed.] 1981)
KEITH M. BROWN, *Kingdom or Province? Scotland and the Royal Union
        1603–1715* (London 1992)
PATRICK S. HODGE (ed.), *Scotland and the Union* (Hume Papers on Public
        Policy vol 2 no 2) (Edinburgh 1994)
COLIN KIDD, *Subverting Scotland's Past* (Cambridge 1991)
T. M. DEVINE, *The Transformation of Rural Scotland* (Edinburgh 1994)
DAVID ALLAN, *Virtue, Learning and the Scottish Enlightenment* (Edinburgh
        1994)
DANIEL SZECHI, *The Jacobites* (Manchester 1994)
JOHN ROBERTSON (ed.), *A Union for Empire* (Cambridge 1995)

For the more modern period there are the three volumes of *People and
Society in Scotland*, vol 1 for 1760–1830 edited by T. M. Devine and
Rosalind Mitchison (Edinburgh 1988), vol 2 for 1830–1914 edited by W.
Hamish Fraser and R. J. Morris (Edinburgh 1990), and vol 3 for 1914–1990
edited by A. Dickson and J. H. Treble (Edinburgh 1992
There is a wealth of literature on nineteenth-century Scotland, from which
only a small selection can be offered. An important book, difficult to get
hold of, is
J. SAUNDERS, *Scottish Democracy* (Edinburgh 1930).

More recent work shows the range of current interests:
R. D. ANDERSON, *Education and Opportunity in Victorian Scotland* (Oxford 1983)
I. CARTER, *Farm Life in North-East Scotland 1840-1914* (Edinburgh 1979)
A. C. CHEYNE, *The Transformation of the Church* (Edinburgh 1983)
T. M. DEVINE, *The Great Highland Famine* (Edinburgh 1988)
I. G. C. HUTCHINSON, *Political History of Scotland 1832-1924* (Edinburgh 1986)
IAN LEVITT, *Poverty and Welfare in Scotland 1890-1948* (Edinburgh 1988) and *Government and Social Conditions in Scotland 1841–1919* (Edinburgh 1988)
A. ALLAN MACKAREN (ed.), *Social Class in Scotland* (Edinburgh 1976)
M. S. MOSS and R. HUME *Workshop of the British Empire. Engineering and Shipbuilding in the West of Scotland* (London 1976)

There is also, of special relevance to the purpose of this book:
MARINELL ASH, *The Strange Death of Scottish History* (Edinburgh 1980)

Some special studies of value for the twentieth century are:
CAIRNS CRAIG, *The History of Scottish Literature* vol 4, *Twentieth Century* (Aberdeen 1988)
DUNCAN MACMILLAN, *Scottish Art 1460-1990* (Edinburgh 1990)
T. C. SMOUT, 'Scotland 1850-1950' in F. M. L. Thompson (ed.), *The Cambridge Social History of Britain 1750-1950* vol 1 (Cambridge 1990)
T. C. SMOUT, *A Century of the Scottish People 1830-1950* (London 1986)

Since 1976 there has been the annual publication of the *Yearbook of Scottish Government* (Edinburgh), edited at first by H. M. DRUCKER and M. G. CLARKE, and later by A. BROWN and D. MCCRONE.

Some Saltire Publications

Geoffrey Barrow, *Robert the Bruce and the Scottish Identity*	0 85411 027 5	£1.00
I. B. Cowan, *Mary Queen of Scots*	0 85411 037 2	£2.50
David Stevenson, *The Covenanters*	0 85411 042 9	£2.95
Kenneth MacKinnon, *Gaelic: a Past and Future Prospect*	0 85411 047 X	£7.95
Meston, Sellars and Cooper, *The Scottish Legal Tradition* (new edition)	0 85411 045 3	£5.99
William Neill, *Tales frae the Odyssey o Homer owreset intil Scots*	0 85411 049 6	£7.99
William Ferguson, *Scotland's Relations with England: a Survey to 1707*	0 85411 058 5	£12.99
Paul Scott, *Andrew Fletcher and the Treaty of Union*	0 85411 057 7	£12.99
Paul Scott, *Walter Scott and Scotland*	0 85411 056 9	£7.99
David Daiches *Robert Burns the Poet*	0 85411 060 7	£12.99
David Stevenson, *Highland Warrior: Alasdair MacColla and the Civil Wars*	0 85411 059 3	£12.99
David Daiches, *et al., The Scottish Enlightenment 1730-1790: a Hotbed of Genius*	0 85411 069 0	£14.99
John Sibbald Gibson, *Edinburgh in the '45: Bonnie Prince Charlie at Holyroodhouse*	0 85411 067 4	£7.99
Thorbjörn Campbell, *Standing Witnesses: an Illustrated Guide to the Scottish Covenanters*	0 85411 061 5	£16.99

Saltire New Poetry

Raymond Vettese, *A Keen New Air*	0 85411 063 1	£7.99

Forthcoming Editions

David Purves, *Grammar and Usage in Scots*	0 85411 068 2
J Derrick McClure, *Why Scots Matters* (new edition)	0 85411 071 2
Ian Grimble, *The World of Rob Donn* (new edition)	0 85411 062 3

Membership details from:
Saltire Society, 9 Fountain Close, High Street, Edinburgh EH1 1TF